"十三五"应用型人才培养规划教材

会计专业英语

Professional English for Accounting

第二版

齐 珺 臧振霞 主编

化学工业出版社

·北京·

《会计专业英语》作为"会计国际化专业教学标准研究"的课题成果,共分为十章。第一至第四章主要讲述会计的性质以及会计信息产生过程;第五至第九章主要讲述关于资产、负债和所有者权益的确认、计量和报告;第十章是关于有关企业经营活动对会计报表的影响,以及如何编制会计报表。

　　本书课后配有案例分析,供读者练习;为了拓展学生的知识面,提升学生的专业修养,本书每课课后增加拓展阅读,主要讲述会计的基本理论及当前的经济热点。

　　本书适用于应用型本科高职高专院校会计及相关专业的学生学习使用,同时还可供从事相关专业的读者阅读参考。

图书在版编目(CIP)数据

会计专业英语/齐珺,臧振霞主编. —2版. —北京:化学工业出版社,2020.1(2024.2重印)
ISBN 978-7-122-35436-5

Ⅰ.①会… Ⅱ.①齐…②臧… Ⅲ.①会计-英语-高等职业教育-教材 Ⅳ.①F23

中国版本图书馆 CIP 数据核字(2019)第 244207 号

责任编辑:蔡洪伟　王　可　　　　装帧设计:刘丽华
责任校对:宋　夏

出版发行:化学工业出版社(北京市东城区青年湖南街13号　邮政编码100011)
印　　装:北京科印技术咨询服务有限公司数码印刷分部
787mm×1092mm　1/16　印张 9¼　字数 224 千字　2024年2月北京第2版第3次印刷

购书咨询:010-64518888　　　　售后服务:010-64518899
网　　址:http://www.cip.com.cn
凡购买本书,如有缺损质量问题,本社销售中心负责调换。

定　　价:38.00元　　　　　　　　　　　　　　　　　　版权所有　违者必究

前言

在世界经济走向一体化之际，会计作为商业语言在商贸交往中起着不可替代的作用，社会对会计人员的要求越来越高。会计人员除了应懂得外语，还要熟悉国际会计惯例，并需具有较广博的国际社会文化背景知识。提高学生的创新能力、职业判断能力和解决实际问题的能力，加快复合型会计人才的培养，已成为相关院校会计教育的当务之急。《会计专业英语》着眼于培养具有良好的外语能力及知识结构的国际化会计人才，因此应改革会计英语的教学方法，调整教育内容，让学生拓宽知识面，不断更新知识，以适应日新月异的客观环境的需要。

本教材在编写时注重国际会计准则与中国会计准则的结合，集会计基础和财务会计实务为一体，体系完整，结构合理，通俗易懂，深入浅出，适用面广；内容充实，习题丰富，难易适中；案例具体，解释详细，思路清晰。本教材不仅适合应用型本科、高职高专院校会计专业的学生学习，还适合有初步会计基础的社会人士进行自学。

全书共十章，齐珺、臧振霞、边国红、王伟参与编写，臧振霞负责统稿。

限于编者水平，书中定有疏漏，恳请理解并提出宝贵意见。

编者
2019 年 6 月

Unit 1 Accounting: Its Foundation — 1

Learning Objectives ········· 1
1.1 What Is Accounting? ········· 1
1.2 Who Uses Accounting Data ········· 1
1.3 Accounting Conventions or Assumptions ········· 3
1.4 Basic Accounting Equation ········· 4
1.5 Effects of Changes in the Economic Business on the Accounting Equation ········· 5
1.6 Financial Statement ········· 10
Key Words and Expressions ········· 13
Exercises ········· 13
Extended Reading ········· 14

Unit 2 The Recording Process — 15

Learning Objectives ········· 15
2.1 Double Entry ········· 15
2.2 The Account ········· 16
2.3 Debits and Credits ········· 17
2.4 Steps in the Recording Process ········· 21
2.5 The Journal ········· 22
2.6 The Ledger ········· 23
2.7 Posting ········· 25
2.8 The Trial Balance ········· 26
Key Words and Expressions ········· 28
Exercises ········· 29
Extended Reading ········· 30

Unit 3 Adjusting the Accounts — 32

Learning Objectives ········· 32
3.1 Accrual-Basis VS. Cash-Basis Accounting ········· 32

3. 2　The Basics of Adjusting Entries ……………………………………… 33
3. 3　Types of Adjusting Entries …………………………………………… 34
3. 4　Adjusting Entries for Prepayments …………………………………… 35
3. 5　Adjusting Entries for Accruals ………………………………………… 39
3. 6　The Adjusted Trial Balance …………………………………………… 47
Key Words and Expressions ………………………………………………… 48
Exercises …………………………………………………………………… 49
Extended Reading ………………………………………………………… 50

Unit 4　Completion of the Accounting Cycle　52

Learning Objectives ………………………………………………………… 52
4. 1　Preparing Closing Entries …………………………………………… 53
4. 2　Preparing Post-closing Trial Balance ………………………………… 55
4. 3　Correcting Entries—an Avoidable Step ……………………………… 59
4. 4　Classified Balance Sheet ……………………………………………… 61
Key Words and Expressions ………………………………………………… 66
Exercises …………………………………………………………………… 66
Extended Reading ………………………………………………………… 67

Unit 5　Current Assets　68

Learning Objectives ………………………………………………………… 68
5. 1　Cash and Cash Equivalents ………………………………………… 68
5. 2　Accounts Receivable ………………………………………………… 72
5. 3　Inventory ……………………………………………………………… 78
Key Words and Expressions ………………………………………………… 85
Exercises …………………………………………………………………… 86
Extended Reading ………………………………………………………… 88

Unit 6　Long-Term Assets　90

Learning Objectives ………………………………………………………… 90
6. 1　Plant and Equipment(Fixed Assets) ………………………………… 90
6. 2　Intangible Assets ……………………………………………………… 96
Key Words and Expressions ………………………………………………… 99
Exercises …………………………………………………………………… 99
Extended Reading ………………………………………………………… 100

Unit 7　Liabilities　102

Learning Objectives ………………………………………………………… 102
7. 1　Current Liabilities …………………………………………………… 102

7.2 Long-term Liabilities	106
Key Words and Expressions	110
Exercises	111
Extended Reading	111

Unit 8 Owner's Equity — 113

Learning Objectives	113
8.1 Accounting for Single Proprietorship	113
8.2 Accounting for Corporation	114
Key Words and Expressions	119
Exercises	120
Extended Reading	121

Unit 9 Measurement of Bussiness Income — 122

Learning Objectives	122
9.1 Revenue	122
9.2 Expense	125
9.3 Business Income	127
Key Words and Expressions	128
Exercises	128
Extended Reading	129

Unit 10 Financial Statements — 130

Learning Objectives	130
10.1 Balance Sheet	130
10.2 Income Statement	132
10.3 The Statement of Owner's Equity	135
10.4 The Statement of Cash Flows	135
Key Words and Expressions	137
Exercises	137
Extended Reading	138

List of Reference Books — 140

Unit 1

Accounting: Its Foundation

Learning Objectives

After studying this unit, you should be able to:
1. Explain what accounting is;
2. Identify the users and uses of accounting;
3. Explain the accounting conventions or assumptions;
4. State the basic accounting equation;
5. Analyze the effects of business transactions on the basic accounting equation;
6. Understand what the three financial statements are and how they are prepared.

1.1 What Is Accounting?

Accounting is an information system that **identifies**, **records**, and **communicates** the economic events of an organization to interested users.

The accounting process may be summarized as follows.

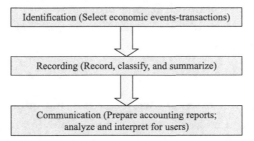

In accounting you should consider the needs of the users of financial information. Therefore, you should know who these users are and what information they need.

1.2 Who Uses Accounting Data

Because it communicates financial information, accounting is often called "the language of business". The information that a user of financial information needs depends upon the kinds of decisions the user makes. The differences in the decisions divide the users of financial information into two broad groups: internal users and external users.

1.2.1 Internal Users

Internal users of accounting information are managers who plan, organize, and run a business. These include **marketing managers, production supervisors, finance directors**, and **company officers**. In running a business, managers must answer many important questions, as shown in the following illustrations.

What is the cost of manufacturing each unit of product?

Can we afford to give employees a pay raise this year?

Which product line is the most profitable?

To answer these and other questions, users need detailed information on a timely basis. For internal users, accounting provides **internal reports**. Examples are financial comparisons of operating alternatives, projections of income from new sales campaigns, and forecasts of cash needs for the next year. In addition, summarized financial information is presented in the form of financial statements.

1.2.2 External Users

There are several types of **external users** of accounting information. **Investors** (owners) use accounting information to make decisions to buy, hold, or sell stock. Creditors such as suppliers and bankers use accounting information to evaluate the risks of granting credit or lending money. Some questions that may be asked by investors and creditors about a company are shown in the following illustrations.

Is the company earning satisfactory income?

How does the company compare in size and profitability with competitors?

The information needs and questions of other external users vary considerably. **Taxing authorities**, such as the Internal Revenue Service, want to know whether the company complies with the tax laws. **Regulatory agencies**, such as the Securities and Exchange Commission and the Federal Trade Commission, want to know whether the company is operating within prescribed rules. **Customers** are interested in whether a company will continue to honor product warranties and support its product lines. **Labor unions** want to know whether the owners can pay increased wages and benefits. **Economic planners** use accounting information to forecast economic activity.

1.3 Accounting Conventions or Assumptions

1.3.1 Accounting Entity Convention

The accounting or financial information of the business is always treated as a separate unit or body from the owner's personal financial information.

The business exists separately from the owner.

It requires that the activities of the entity be kept separate and distinct from the activities of its owner and all other economic entities.

For example, the owner has a business, which includes a warehouse and trucks used in the business, and these are both recorded (or shown) in the books of the business. However, the house where the owner lives and the boat that is used on the weekend is personal property and is not shown (or recorded) in the books of the business. Also, the bank account of the business is to be kept separate from any personal or private bank accounts.

In accounting, the owner is treated as separate from the business. In a court of law, however, the owner of the business may not always be treated as separate from the business.

1.3.2 Accounting Period Convention

The life of a business, however long it lasts, is broken into equal periods of at least one year.

The accounting or financial reports are prepared for a specific period of time to enable two things: an assessment of the results from the buying and selling of goods, and a meaningful comparison with expected or past results.

1.3.3 Going Concern Convention

It is also called Continuity of Activity Convention. Financial reports or statements are prepared on the assumption that the life of the business will continue indefinitely. A business is regarded as a going concern as long as it can pay its bills when they have to be paid and the intention of the owner is not to cease business but to carry on with that business.

A business is started because the owner expects it to be successful and to earn adequate profits. Even when the owner wants to retire, there may be an expectation that the business will be sold and will carry on indefinitely into the future.

1.3.4 Monetary Unit Convention

The monetary unit convention requires that only transaction data that can be expressed in terms of money be included in the accounting records. This assumption enables accounting to quantify (measure) economic events. This assumption does prevent some relevant information from being included in the accounting records.

If a monetary value can not be given to a transaction, then it cannot be recorded in the books of the business, or eventually, be included in an accounting financial statement or report.

The sale of 1,000 goods or items for $5.00 each is recorded as sales of $5,000. The 1,000 units are not shown, only the monetary value of those units.

An important part of the monetary unit assumption is the added assumption that the unit of measure remains sufficiently constant over time. However, the assumption of a stable monetary unit has been challenged because of the significant decline in the purchasing power of the dollar. For example, what used to cost $1.00 in 1960 dollars over $4.00 in 2001 dollars is highly questionable. The profession has recognized this problem and encourages companies to disclose the effects of changing prices.

1.4 Basic Accounting Equation

Other essential building blocks of accounting are the categories into which economic events are classified. The two basic elements of a business are what it owns and what it owes. Assets are the resources owned by a business. The relationship of assets, liabilities, and owner's equity can be expressed as an equation as follows.

$$\boxed{\text{Assets}} = \boxed{\text{Liabilities}} + \boxed{\text{Owner's Equity}}$$

This relationship is referred to as the basic accounting equation. Assets must equal the sum of liabilities and owner's equity. Because creditors' claims must be paid before ownership claims if a business is liquidated, liabilities are shown before owner's equity in the basic accounting equation.

The accounting equation applies to all economic entities regardless of size, nature of business, or form of business organization. It applies to a small proprietorship such as a corner grocery store as well as to a giant corporation. The equation provides the underlying framework for recording and summarizing the economic events of a business enterprise.

1.5 Effects of Changes in the Economic Business on the Accounting Equation

Transactions (often referred to as business transactions) are the economic events of an enterprise that are recorded. Transactions may be identified as external or internal. **External transactions involve economic events between the company and some outside enterprise.** A company may carry on many activities that do not in themselves represent business transactions. Hiring employees, answering the telephone, talking with customers, and placing orders for merchandise are examples. Some of these activities, however, may lead to business transactions: Employees will earn wages, and merchandise will be delivered by suppliers. Each event must be analyzed to find out if it has an effect on the components of the basic accounting equation. If it does, it will be recorded in the accounting process.

The equality of the basic equation must be preserved. Therefore, each transaction must have a dual effect on the equation. For example, if an asset is increased, there must be a corresponding:

(1) Decrease in another asset, or

(2) Increase in a specific liability, or

(3) Increase in owner's equity.

It follows that two or more items could be affected when an asset is increased. For example, as one asset is increased $10,000, another asset could decrease $6,000 and a specific liability could increase $4,000. Any change in a liability or ownership claim is subject to similar analysis.

The following examples are business transactions for a computer programming business during its first month of operations. You will want to study these transactions until you are sure you understand them. They are not difficult, but they are important to your success in this course. The ability to analyze transactions in terms of the basic accounting equation is essential for an understanding of accounting.

1.5.1 Transaction: Investment by Owner

Ray Neal decides to open a computer programming service which he names **Softbyte**. On September 1, 2017, he invests $15,000 cash in the business. This transaction results in an equal increase in assets and owner's equity. The asset Cash increases $15,000, as does the owner's equity identified as R. Neal, Capital. The effect of this transaction on the basic equation is:

$$\boxed{\text{Assets}} = \boxed{\text{Liabilities}} + \boxed{\text{Owner's Equity}}$$

Cash: +$15,000=Capital: +$15,000

Observe that the equality of the basic equation has been maintained. Note also that the source of the increase in owner's equity (Investment) is indicated. Why does this matter? Because investments by the owner do not represent revenues, and they are excluded in determining net income, therefore it is necessary to make clear that the increase is an investment rather than revenue from operations.

	Assets	=	Liabilities	+	Owner's Equity
	Cash	=			R. Neal, Capital
Bal.	$15,000				$15,000

1.5.2 Transaction: Purchase of Equipment for Cash

Softbyte purchases computer equipment for $7,000 cash. This transaction results in an equal increase and decrease in total assets, though the composition of assets changes: Cash is decreased $7,000, and the asset Equipment is increased $7,000. The specific effect of this transaction and cumulative effect of the first two transactions are:

	Assets		=	Liabilities	+	Owner's Equity
	Cash +	Equipment	=			R. Neal, Capital $15,000
Old Bal.	$15,000					
	−$7,000	+$7,000				
New Bal.	$8,000	$7,000				
	$15,000		=			$15,000

Observe that total assets are still $15,000, and Neal's equity also remains at $15,000, the amount of his original investment.

1.5.3 Transaction: Purchase of Supplies on Credit

Softbyte purchases for $1,600 from Pioneer Supply Company computer paper and other supplies expected to last several months. Acme agrees to allow **Softbyte** to pay this bill next month, in October. This transaction is referred to as a purchase on account or a credit purchase. Assets are increased because of the expected future benefits of using the paper and supplies, and liabilities are increased by the amount due Acme Company. The asset Supplies is increased $1,600 and the liability Accounts Payable is increased by the same amount. The effect on the equation is:

	Assets			=	Liabilities	+	Owner's Equity
	Cash +	Supplies +	Equipment	=	Accounts Payable		R. Neal, Capital
Old Bal.	$8,000		$7,000				$15,000
		+$1,600			+$1,600		
New Bal.	$8,000 +	$1,600 +	$7,000	=	$1,600	+	$15,000
	$16,600				$16,600		

Total assets are now $16,600. This total is matched by a $1,600 creditor's claim and a $15,000 ownership claim.

1.5.4 Transaction: Services Provided for Cash

Softbyte receives $1,200 cash from customers for programming services it has provided. This transaction represents **Softbyte's** principal revenue-producing activity. Recall that revenue increases owner's equity. In this transaction, Cash is increased $1,200, and R. Neal, Capital is increased $1,200. The new balances in the equation are:

	Assets			=	Liabilities	+	Owner's Equity
	Cash	+ Supplies	+ Equipment	=	Accounts Payable	+	R. Neal, Capital
Old Bal.	$8,000 +$1,200	+ $1,600	+ $7,000	=	$1,600	+	$15,000 +$1,200(Revenue)
New Bal.	$9,200	+ $1,600	+ $7,000	=	$1,600	+	$16,200
	$17,800				$17,800		

The two sides of the equation balance at $17,800. The source of the increase in owner's equity is indicated as Service Revenue. Service Revenue is included in determining **Softbyte's** net income.

1.5.5 Transaction: Purchase of Advertising on Credit

Softbyte receives a bill for $250 from the *Daily News* for advertising but postpones payment of the bill until a later date. This transaction results in an increase in liabilities and a decrease in owner's equity. The specific items involved are Accounts Payable and R. Neal, Capital. The effect on the equation is:

	Assets			=	Liabilities	+	Owner's Equity
	Cash	+ Supplies	+ Equipment	=	Accounts Payable	+	R. Neal, Capital
Old Bal.	$9,200	+ $1,600	+ $7,000	=	$1,600 +$250	+	$16,200 −$250(Expense)
New Bal.	$9,200	+ $1,600	+ $7,000	=	$1,850	+	$15,950
	$17,800				$17,800		

The two sides of the equation still balance at $17,800. Owner's equity is decreased when the expense is incurred, and the specific cause of the decrease (Advertising Expense) is noted, expenses do not have to be paid in cash at the time they are incurred. When payment is made at a later date, the liability Accounts Payable will be decreased and the asset Cash will be decreased. The cost of advertising is considered an expense, as opposed to an asset because the benefits have been used. This expense is included in determining net income.

1.5.6 Transaction: Services Provided for Cash and Credit

Softbyte provides $3,500 of programming services for customers. Cash of $1,500 is received from customers, and the balance of $2,000 is billed on account. This transaction results in an equal increase in assets and owner's equity. The new balances are as follows.

	Assets				=	Liabilities	+	Owner's Equity
	Cash +	Receivable +	Supplies +	Equipment	=	Accounts Payable	+	R. Neal, Capital
Old Bal.	$9,200		+ $1,600	+ $7,000	=	$1,850	+	$15,950
	+$1,500	+ $2,000						+$3,500(Revenue)
New Bal.	$10,700	+ $2,000	+ $1,600	+ $7,000	=	$1,850	+	$19,450
	$21,300					$21,300		

Why is owner's equity increased $3,500 when only $1,500 has been collected? Because the inflow of assets resulting from the earning of revenues does not have to be in the form of cash. Remember that owner's equity is increased when revenues are earned. In **Softbyte's** case revenues are earned when the service is provided. When collections on account are received later, Cash will be increased and Accounts Receivable will be decreased.

1.5.7 Transaction: Payment of Expenses

Expenses paid in cash for September are store rent $600, salaries of employees $900, and utilities $200. These payments result in an equal decrease in assets and owner's equity. Cash is decreased $1,700, and R. Neal, Capital is decreased by the same amount. The effect of these payments on the equation is:

	Assets				=	Liabilities	+	Owner's Equity
	Cash +	Receivable +	Supplies +	Equipment	=	Accounts Payable	+	R. Neal, Capital
Old Bal.	$10,700 +	$2,000	+ $1,600	+ $7,000	=	$1,850	+	$19,450
	−$1,700							−$1,700(Expense)
New Bal.	$9,000 +	$2,000	+ $1,600	+ $7,000	=	$1,850	+	$17,750
	$19,600					$19,600		

1.5.8 Transaction: Payment of Accounting Payable

Softbyte pays its $250 *Daily News* advertising bill in cash. Remember that the bill was previously recorded as an increase in Accounts Payable and a decrease in owner's equity. This payment "on account" decreases the asset Cash by $250 and also decreases the liability Accounts Payable by $250. The effect of this transaction on the equation is:

	Assets				=	Liabilities	+	Owner's Equity
	Cash +	Receivable +	Supplies +	Equipment	=	Accounts Payable	+	R.Neal, Capital
Old Bal.	$9,000 +	$2,000	+ $1,600	+ $7,000	=	$1,850	+	$17,750
	−$250					−$250		
New Bal.	$8,750 +	$2,000	+ $1,600	+ $7,000	=	$1,600	+	$17,750
	$19,350					$19,350		

Observe that the payment of a liability related to an expense that has previously been recorded does not affect owner's equity.

1.5.9 Transaction: Receipt of Cash on Account

The sum of $600 in cash is received from customers who have previously been billed for services. This transaction does not change total assets, but it changes the composition of those assets. Cash is increased $600 and Accounts Receivable is decreased $600. The new balances are:

	Assets				=	Liabilities	+	Owner's Equity
	Cash +	Receivable +	Supplies +	Equipment	=	Accounts Payable		R. Neal, Capital
Old Bal.	$8,750	$2,000	$1,600	$7,000	=	$1,600		$17,750
	+$600	−$600						
New Bal.	$9,350 +	$1,400 +	$1,600 +	$7,000	=	$1,600	+	$17,750
		$19,350					$19,350	

Note that a collection on account for services previously billed and recorded does not affect owner's equity.

1.5.10 Transaction: Withdrawal of Cash by Owner

Ray Neal withdraws $1,300 in cash from the business for his personal use. This transaction results in an equal decrease in assets and owner's equity. Both Cash and R. Neal, Capital are decreased $1,300 as shown below.

	Assets				=	Liabilities	+	Owner's Equity
	Cash +	Receivable +	Supplies +	Equipment	=	Accounts Payable		R. Neal, Capital
Old Bal.	$9,350 +	$1,400 +	$1,600 +	$7,000	=	$1,600		$17,750
	−$1,300							−$1,300(Drawings)
New Bal.	$8,050 +	$1,400 +	$1,600 +	$7,000	=	$1,600	+	$16,450
		$18,050					$18,050	

Observe that the effect of a cash withdrawal by the owner is the opposite of the effect of an investment by the owner. Owner's drawings are not expenses. Like owner's investment, they are excluded in determining net income.

1.5.11 Summary of Transactions

The September transactions of **Softbyte** are summarized below. The transaction number, the specific effects of the transaction, and the balances after each transaction are indicated. The following illustration demonstrates some significant facts.

(1) Each transaction must be analyzed in terms of its effect on:
① The three components of the basic accounting equation.
② Specific types (kinds) of items within each component.
(2) The two sides of the equation must always be equal.
(3) The causes of each change in the owner's claim on assets must be indicated in the owner's equity column.

There! You made it through transaction analysis. If you feel a bit shaky on any of the transactions, it might be a good idea at this point to get up, take a short break, and come back again for a 10- to 15-minute review of the transactions, to make sure you understand them before you go on to the next section.

Transaction	Assets				=	Liabilities	+	Owner's Equity
	Cash	+ Receivable	+ Supplies	+ Equipment	=	Accounts Payable	+	R. Neal, Capital
(1)	+15,000							15,000(Investment)
(2)	−7,000			+ 7,000				
	8,000	+		7,000	=			15,000
(3)								
	8,000		+ 1,600	+ 7,000	=	1,600	+	15,000
(4)	+1,200				=		+	1,200
	9,200	+	1,600	+ 7,000	=	1,600	+	16,200
(5)						+ 250	−	250
	9,200	+	1,600	+ 7,000	=	1,850	+	15,950
(6)	+1,500	+ 2,000					+	3,500
	10,700	+ 2,000	+ 1,600	+ 7,000	=	1,850	+	19,450
(7)	−1,700						−	1,700
	9,000	+ 2,000	+ 1,600	+ 7,000	=	1,850	+	17,750
(8)	−250					− 250		
	8,750	+ 2,000	+ 1,600	+ 7,000	=	1,600	−	17,750
(9)	+600	−600						
	9,350	1,400	1,600	7,000	=	1,600	−	17,750
(10)	−1,300							−1,300
	8,050	+ 1,400	+ 1,600	+ 7,000	=	1,600	−	16,450

1.6 Financial Statement

After transactions are identified, recorded, and summarized, financial statements are prepared from the summarized accounting data:

(1) An income statement presents the revenues and resulting net income or net loss for a specific period of time.

(2) An owner's equity statement summarizes the changes in owner's equity for a specific period of time.

(3) A balance sheet reports the assets, liabilities, and owner's equity at a specific date.

Each statement provides management, owners, and other interested parties with relevant financial date.

Be sure to carefully examine the format and content of each statement.

1.6.1 Income Statement

Softbyte's income statement reports the revenues and expenses for a specific period of time (in this case, "For the Month Ended September 30, 2017"). Its income statement is prepared for the date appearing in the owner's equity column. On the income statement, revenues are listed first, followed by expenses. Finally net income (or net loss) is determined.

Note that investment and withdrawal transactions between the owner and the business are not included in the measurement of net income. For example, the withdrawal by Ray Neal of cash from **Softbyte** was not regarded as a business expense.

SOFTBYTE
Income Statement
For the Month Ended September 30, 2017

Revenues
Service revenue $ 4,700
Expenses
Salaries expense $ 900
Rent expense 600
Advertising expense 250
Utilities expense 200
Total expense $ 1,950
Net Income $ 2,750

1.6.2 Owner's Equity Statement

Softbyte's owner's equity statement reports the changes in owner's equity for a specific period of time. The time period is the same as that covered by the income statement. Data for the preparation of the owner's equity statement are obtained from the owner's equity column of the tabular summary and from the income statement. The beginning owner's equity amount is shown on the first line of the statement. Then, the owner's investments, net income, and the owner's drawings are identified. The information in this statement indicates the reasons why owner's equity has increased or decreased during the period.

SOFTBYTE
Owner's Equity Statement
For the Month Ended September 30, 2017

R. Neal, Capital, September 1		$ 0
Add: Investments	$ 15,000	
Net income	2,750	17,750
		17,750
Less: Drawings		1,300
R. Neal, Capital, September 30		$ 16,450

What if **Softbyte** in its first month? Let's assume that during the month of September 2017, **Softbyte** lost $ 10,000. The presentation in the owner's equity statement of a net loss appears as follows.

SOFTBYTE
Owner's Equity Statement
For The Month Ended September 30, 2017

R. Neal, Capital, September 1 $ 0

Add: Investments	15,000
	15,000
Less: Drawings	$1,300
Net loss	10,000
	11,300
R. Neal, Capital, September 30	$3,700

Any additional investments are reported as investments in the owner's equity statement.

1.6.3 Balance Sheet

Softbyte's balance sheet reports the assets, liabilities, and owner's equity at a specific date (in this case, September 30, 2017). The balance sheet is prepared from the column headings and the month-end data shown in the last line of the tabular summary. Observe that the assets are listed at the top, followed by liabilities and owner's equity assets must equal total liability, accounts payable is reported.

SOFTBYTE
Balance Sheet
September 30, 2017
Assets

Cash	$8,050
Accounts Receivable	1,400
Supplies	1,600
Equipment	7,000
Total assets	$18,050

Liabilities and Owner's Equity

Liabilities	
Accounts Payable	$1,600
Owner's Equity	
R. Neal, Capital	16,450
Total liabilities and owner's equity	$18,050

In most cases, there will be more than one liability. When two or more liabilities are involved, a customary way of listing is as follows.

Liabilities	
Notes payable	$10,000
Accounts payable	$63,000
Salaries payable	$18,000
Total liabilities	$91,000

The balance sheet is like a snapshot of the company's financial condition at a specific moment in time (usually the month-end or year-end).

Key Words and Expressions

1. accounting — 会计
2. financial information — 财务信息
3. internal user — 内部使用者
4. external user — 外部使用者
5. financial statement — 财务报告
6. creditor — 债权人
7. investor — 投资者
8. accounting assumption — 会计假设
9. accounting entity — 会计主体
10. accounting period — 会计分期
11. going concern — 持续经营
12. monetary unit — 货币计量
13. accounting equation — 会计等式
14. asset — 资产
15. liability — 负债
16. owner's equity — 所有者权益
17. transaction — 交易
18. economic event — 经济活动
19. purchase on credit — 赊购
20. expense — 费用
21. revenue — 收入
22. profit — 利润
23. withdrawal — 提款
24. balance sheet — 资产负债表
25. income statement — 利润表
26. net income — 净收益
27. accounts payable — 应付账款

Exercises

Case 1

At the beginning of the year, Gills Company had total assets of $820,000 and total liabilities of $500,000. Answer the following questions.

(1) If total assets increased $150,000 during the year and total liabilities deceased $80,000, what is the amount of owner's equity at the end of the year?

(2) During the year, total liabilities increased $100,000 and owner's equity decreased $70,000, what is the amount of total assets at the end of the year?

(3) If total assets decreased $90,000 and owner's equity $120,000 during the year, what is the amount of total liabilities at the end of the year?

Case 2

Kidman Computer Timeshare Company entered into the following transactions during May 2017.

(1) Purchased computer terminals for $21,500 from Digital Equipment on account.

(2) Paid $4,000 cash for May rent on storage space.

(3) Received $15,000 cash from customers for contracts billed in April.

(4) Provided computer services to Fisher Construction Company for $3,000 cash.

(5) Paid Northern States Power Co. $11,000 cash for energy usage in May.

(6) Kidman invested an additional $32,000 in the business.

(7) Paid Digital Equipment for the terminals purchased in (1) above.

(8) Incurred advertising expense for May of $1,200 on account.

Instructions

Indicate with the appropriate letter whether each of the transactions above result in:

(1) an increase in assets and a decrease in assets.

(2) an increase in assets and an increase in owner's equity.

(3) an increase in assets and an increase in liabilities.

(4) a decrease in assets and a decrease in owner's equity.

(5) a decrease in assets and a decrease in liabilities.

(6) an increase in liabilities and a decrease in owner's equity.

(7) an increase in owner's equity and a decrease in liabilities.

Extended Reading

Distinguishing Between Bookkeeping and Accounting

Many individuals mistakenly consider bookkeeping and accounting to be the same. This confusion is understandable because the accounting process includes the **bookkeeping function**. However, accounting also includes much more. Bookkeeping **usually involves only the recording of economic events**. It is therefore just one part of the accounting process. In total, **accounting involves the entire process of identifying, recording, and communicating economic events**.

Accounting may be further divided into financial accounting and managerial accounting. Financial accounting is the field of accounting that provides economic and financial information for investors, creditors, and other external users. Managerial accounting provides economic and financial information for managers and other internal users.

Unit 2
The Recording Process

Learning Objectives ▶▶

After studying this unit, you should be able to:
1. Explain what an account is and how it helps in the recording process;
2. Define debits and credits and explain how they are used to record business transactions;
3. Identify the basic steps in the recording process;
4. Explain what a journal is and how it helps in the recording process;
5. Explain what a ledger is and how it helps in the recording process;
6. Explain what posting is and how it helps in the recording process;
7. Prepare a trail balance and explain its purposes.

In Unit 1, we analyzed business transactions in terms of the accounting equation. The cumulative effects of these transactions were presented in tabular form. Imagine a restaurant and gift shop such as The Mug and Musket using the same tabular format as Softbyte to keep track of every one of its transactions. In a single day, this restaurant and gift shop engages in hundreds of business transactions. To record each transaction this way would be impractical, expensive, and unnecessary. Instead, a set of procedures and records are used to keep track of transaction data more easily.

This unit introduces and illustrates these basic procedures and records. The content and organization of Unit 2 are as follows.

2.1 Double Entry

It has been shown that a balance sheet can be used to record transactions. The double entry system that we are now going to look at is very similar because each transaction is recorded twice. Most businesses have to record many transactions each day and would quickly fill even the biggest balance sheet. To allow more room to record transactions, the double entry system keeps a separate record or account of each type of asset and liability. For example, machinery transactions are recorded in a Machinery account; and cash at bank transactions are recorded in a Cash at Bank account.

Each transaction is recorded twice in the double entry system:
- On the left or debit side of one account;
- On the right or credit side of another account.

There are simple rules for deciding when to debit an account and when to credit it:
- To increase an asset, debit the account;
- To decrease an asset, credit the account;
- To increase a liability, credit the account;
- To decrease a liability, debit the account.

It is a good idea to learn these rules by heart before going any further.

Accounts come in different layouts, but the simplest are "T" shaped. These are called T-accounts. Here is an example of two T-accounts, an asset account and a liability account. The accounts are shown with the double entry rules on them:

You will notice that the top of the "T" underlines the account name and the vertical stem of the account separates the debit (left) side from the credit (right) side.

AN ASSET ACCOUNT		A LIABILITY ACCOUNT	
LEFT or "DEBIT" side to record INCREASES	RIGHT or "CREDIT" side to record DECREASES	LEFT or "DEBIT" side to record DECREASES	RIGHT or "CREDIT" side to record INCREASES

2.2 • The Account

An account is an individual accounting record of increases and decreases in a specific asset, liability, or owner's equity item. For example, **Softbyte** (the company discussed in Unit 1) would have separate accounts for Cash, Accounts Receivable, Accounts Payable, Service Revenue, Salaries Expense, and so on. In its simplest form, an account consists of three parts: (1) the title of the account, (2) a left or debit side, and (3) a right or credit side. Because the alignment of these parts of an account resembles the letter T, it is referred to as a **T-account**. The basic form of an account is shown below.

Title of Account

Left or debit side	Right or credit side
Debit balance	Credit balance

T-account

The T-account is standard shorthand in accounting that helps make clear the effects of transactions on individual accounts. We will use it often throughout this book to explain basic accounting relationships. (Note that when we are referring to a specific account, we capitalize its name.)

2.3 Debits and Credits

The term **debit** means left, and **credit** means right. They are commonly abbreviated as Dr. for debit and Cr. for credit. These terms are directional signals: They indicate which side of a T-account a number will be recorded on. Entering an amount on the left side of an account is called **debiting** the account; making an entry on the right side is **crediting** the account.

The procedure of having debits on the left and credits on the right is an accounting custom, or rule (like the custom of driving on the right-hand side of the road in the United States). **This rule applies to all accounts.** When the totals of the two sides are compared, an account will have a **debit balance** if the total of the debit amounts exceeds the credits. An account will have a **credit balance** if the credit amounts exceed the debits.

The recording of debits and credits in an account is shown below for the cash transactions of **Softbyte.** The data are taken from the cash column of the tabular summary in Unit 1.

Tabular Summary	Account Form	
Cash	Cash	
$15,000	(Debits) 15,000	(Credits) 7,000
−7,000	1,200	1,700
1,200	1,500	250
1,500	600	1,300
−1,700	Balance 8,050	
−250	(Debits)	
600		
−1,300		
$8,050		

> **HELPFUL HINT**
> At this point, don't think about increases and decreases in relation to debits and credits. As you'll soon learn, the effects of debits and credits depend on the type of account involved.

In the tabular summary every positive item represents a receipt of cash; every negative amount represents a payment of cash. Notice that in the account form the increases in cash are recorded as debits, and the decreases in cash are recorded as credits. Having increases on one side and decreases on the other helps in determining the total of each side of the account as well as the overall balance in the account. The account balance, a debit of $8,050, indicates that **Softbyte** has had $8,050 more increases than decreases in cash.

2.3.1 Debit and Credit Procedure

In Unit 1 you learned the effect of a transaction on the basic accounting equation. Remember that each transaction must involve two or more accounts to keep the basic accounting equation in balance. In other words, for each transaction debits must be equal to credits in the accounts. The equality of debits and credits provides the basis for the **double-entry system** of recording transaction.

HELPFUL HINT
Debits must be equal to credits for each transaction.

Under the double-entry system the dual (two-sided) effect of each transaction is recorded in appropriate accounts. This universally used system provides a logical method for recording transactions. It also offers a means of proving the accuracy of the recorded amounts. If every transaction is recorded with equal debits and credits, then the sum of all the debits to the accounts must equal the sum of all the credits.

The double-entry system for determining the equality of the accounting equation is much more efficient than the plus/minus procedure used in Unit 1. There, it was necessary after each transaction to compare total assets with total liabilities and owner's equity to determine the equality of the two sides of the accounting equation.

2.3.2 Assets and Liabilities

We know that both sides of the basic equation (Assets=Liabilities+Owner's Equity) must be equal. It follows that increases and decreases in assets and liabilities must be recorded opposite from each other. In the above illustration, increases in cash—an asset—were entered on the left side, and decreases in cash were entered on the right side. Therefore, increases in liabilities must be entered on the right or credit side, and decreases in liabilities must be entered on the left or debit side. The effects that debits and credits have on assets and liabilities are summarized as follows.

Debit and Credit Effects —Assets and Liabilities	
Debits	**Credits**
Increase assets	Decrease assets
Decrease liabilities	Increase liabilities

HELPFUL HINT
The normal balance for an account is always the same as the increase side.

Debits to a specific asset account should exceed the credits to that account. Credits to liability account should exceed debits to that account. The **normal balance** of an account is on the side where an increase in the account is recorded. Thus, asset accounts normally show debit balances, and liability accounts normally show credit balances. The normal balances can be diagrammed as follows.

Normal Balances—Assets and Liabilities

Assets		Liabilities	
Debit for increase	Credit for decrease	Debit for increase	Credit for decrease
Normal balance			Normal balance

Knowing the normal balance in an account may help you trace errors. For example, a credit balance in an asset account such as Land or a debit balance in a liability account such as Wages Payable would indicate recording errors. Occasionally, an abnormal balance may be correct. The Cash account, for example, will have a credit balance when a company has overdrawn its bank balance (i.e., written a "bad" check).

2.3.3 Owner's Equity

As indicated in Unit 1, owner's equity is increased by owner's investments and revenues. It is decreased by owner's drawing and by expenses. In a double-entry system, accounts are kept for each of these types of transactions.

2.3.4 Owner's Capital

Investments by owners are credited to the Owner's Capital account. Credits increase this account and debits decrease it. For example, when cash is invested in the business, Cash is debited (increased) and Owner's Capital is credited (increased). When the owner's investment in the business is reduced, Owner's Capital is debited (decreased).

The rules of debit and credit for the Owner's Capital account are stated as follows.

Debit and Credit Effects—Owner's Capital

Debits	Credits
Decrease Owner's Capital	Increase Owner's Capital

The normal balance in this account can be diagrammed as follows.

Normal Balance—Owner's Capital

Owner's Capital	
Debit for decrease	Credit for increase
	Normal balance

2.3.5 Owner's Drawing

An owner may withdraw cash or other assets for personal use. Withdrawals could be debited directly to Owner's Capital to indicate a decrease in owner's equity. However, it is preferable to establish a separate account, called the Owner's Drawing account. This separate account makes it easier to determine total withdrawals for each accounting period.

The Drawing Account decreases Owner's Equity. It is not an income statement account like revenues and expenses. Owner's Drawing is increased by debits and decreased by credits. Normally, the drawing account will have a debit balance.

The rules of debit and credit for the drawing account are stated as follows.

Debit and Credit Effects—Owner's Drawing

Debits	Credits
Increase Owner's Drawing	Decrease Owner's Drawing

The normal balance can be diagrammed as follows.

Normal Balance—Owner's Drawing

Owner's Drawing	
Debit for increase	Credit for decrease
Normal balance	

2.3.6 Revenues and Expenses

Remember that the ultimate purpose of earning revenues is to benefit the owner(s) of the business. When revenues are earned, owner's equity is increased. Therefore, **the effect of debits and credits on revenue accounts is the same as their effect on Owner's Capital.** Revenue accounts are increased by credits and decreased by debits.

> **HELPFUL HINT**
> Because revenues increase owner's equity, a revenue account has the same debit and credit rules as does the Owner's Capital account. Conversely, expenses have the opposite effect.

Expenses have the opposite effect: decrease owner's equity. Since expenses are the negative factor in computing net income, and revenues are the positive factor, it is logical that the increase and decrease sides of expenses accounts should be the reverse accounts. Thus, expense accounts are increased by debits and decreased by credits.

The effect of debits and credits on revenues and expenses can be stated as follows.

Debit and Credit Effects—Revenues and Expenses

Debits	Credits
Decrease revenues	Increase revenues
Increase expenses	Decrease expenses

Credits to revenue accounts should exceed debits, and debits to expense accounts should exceed credits. Thus, revenue accounts normally show credit balances and expense accounts normally show debit balances. The normal balances can be diagrammed as follows.

Normal Balances—Revenues and Expenses

Revenues		Expenses	
Debit for decrease	Credit for increase	Debit for increase	Credit for decrease
	Normal balance	Normal balance	

2.3.7 Expansion Basic Equation

You have already learned the basic accounting equation. The following expands this equation to rules and effects on each type of account are illustrated. Study this diagram carefully. It will help you understand the fundamentals of the double-entry system. Like the basic equation, the expanded basic equation must be in balance (total debits equal to credits).

Expanded Basic Equation and Debit/Credit Rules and Effects

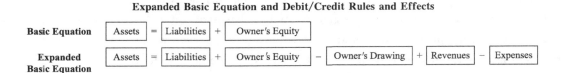

2.4 Steps in the Recording Process

In practically every business, the basic steps in the recording process are:
(1) Analyze each transaction for its effects on the accounts.
(2) Enter the transaction information in a journal (book of original entry).
(3) Transfer the journal information to the appropriate accounts in the ledger (book of accounts).

Although it is possible to enter transaction information directly into the accounts without using a journal or ledger, few businesses do so.

The sequence of events in the recording process begins with the transaction. Evidence of the transaction is provided by a **business document**, such as a sales slip, a check, a bill, or a cash register tape. This evidence is analyzed to determine the effects of the transaction on specific accounts. The transaction is then entered in the journal. Finally, the journal entry is transferred to the designated accounts in the ledger. The sequence of events in the recording process is shown below.

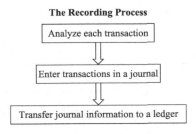

The basic steps in the recording process occur repeatedly. The analysis of transactions was illustrated in Unit 1. Further examples will be given in this and later units. The other steps in the recording process are explained in the following sections.

2.5 The Journal

Transactions are initially recorded in chronological order in a **journal** before being transferred to the accounts. Thus, the journal is referred to as the book of original entry. For each transaction the journal shows the debit and credit effects on specific accounts. Companies may use various kinds of journals, but every company has the most basic form of journal, a **general journal**. Typically, a general journal has spaces for dates, account titles and explanations, references, and two amount columns. Whenever we use the term journal in this textbook without a modifying adjective, we mean the general journal.

The journal makes several significant contributions to the recording process:

(1) It discloses in one place the complete effects of a transaction.

(2) It provides a chronological record of transactions.

(3) It helps to prevent or locate errors because the debit and credit amounts for each entry can be readily compared.

Entering transaction data in the journal is known as **journalizing**. Separate journal entries are made for each transaction. A complete entry consists of: (1) the date of the transaction, (2) the accounts and amounts to be debited and credited, and (3) a brief explanation of the transaction.

The following illustration shows the technique of journalizing, using the first two transactions of **Softbyte**. These transactions are: September 1, Ray Neal invested $15,000 cash in the business, and computer equipment was purchased for $7,000 cash. The numbered J1 indicates that two entries are recorded on the first page of the journal.

Technique of Journalizing

GENERAL JOURNAL

Date	Account Titles and Explanation	Ref	Debit	Credit
2017				
Sept. 1	Cash		15,000	
	R. Neal, Capital			15,000
	(Owner's investment of cash in business)			
J1	Computer equipment		7,000	
	Cash			7,000
	(Purchase of equipment for cash)			

The standard form and content of journal entries are as follows.

(1) The date of the transaction is entered in the Date column. The date recorded should include the year, month, and day of the transaction.

(2) The debit account title (that is the account to be debited) is entered first at the extreme left margin of the column headed "Account Titles and Explanation", and the amount of the debit is recorded in the Debit column.

(3) The credit account title (that is the account to be credited) is indented and entered on the next line in the column headed "Account Titles and Explanation", and the amount of the credit is recovered in the Credit column.

(4) A brief explanation of the transaction is given on the line below the credit account title.

(5) A space is left between journal entries. The blank spaces between individual journal entries make the entire journal easier to read.

(6) The column title Ref. (which stands for reference) is left blank when the journal entry is made. This column is used later when the journal entries are transferred to the ledger accounts. At that time, the ledger account number is placed in the Reference column to indicate where the amount in the journal entry was transferred.

It is important to use correct and specific account titles in journalizing. Since most accounts appear later in the financial statements, wrong account titles lead to incorrect financial statements. Some flexibility exists initially in selecting account title. The main criterion is that each title must appropriately describe the content of the account. For example, the account title used for the cost of delivery trucks may be Delivery Equipment, Delivery Trucks, or Trucks. Once a company choose the specific title to use, all later transactions involving the account should be recorded under that account title.

If an entry involves only two accounts, one debit and one credit, it is considered a simple entry. Some transactions, however, require more than two accounts in journalizing. When three or more accounts are required in one journal entry, the entry is referred to as a **compound entry**. To illustrate, assume that on July 1, Butler Company purchases a delivery truck costing $14,000 by paying $8,000 cash and the balance on account (to be paid later). The compound entry is as follows.

Compound Journal Entry

GENERAL JOURNAL

Date	Account Titles and Explanation	Ref	Debit	Credit
2017				
July 1	Delivery Equipment		14,000	
	Cash			8,000
	Accounts Payable			6,000
	(Purchase of truck for cash with balance on account)			

HELPFUL HINT
Assume you find this compound entry: Wages Expense 700, Cash 1,200, Advert. Expense 400 (Paid cash for wages and advertising). Is the entry correct? No. It is incorrect in form because both debits should be listed before the credit. It is incorrect in content because the debit amounts do not equal the credit amount.

In a compound entry, the total debit and credit amounts must be equal. Also, the standard format requires that all debits be listed before the credits.

2.6 The Ledger

The entire group of accounts maintained by a company is called the ledger. The ledger keeps in one place all the information about changes in specific account balances.

Companies may use various kinds of ledgers, but every company has a general ledger. A general ledger contains all the assets, liabilities, and owner's equity accounts, as shown below. A business can use a looseleaf binder or card file for the ledger. Each account is kept on a separate sheet or card. Whenever we use the term ledger in this textbook without a modifying adjective, we mean the general ledger.

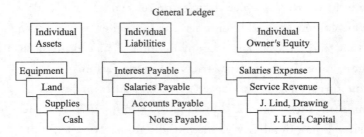

The ledger should be arranged in the order in which accounts are presented in the financial statements. Beginning with the balance sheet accounts, first in order are the asset accounts, followed by liability account, owner's capital, owner's drawing, revenues, and expenses. Each account is numbered for easier identification.

The ledger provides management with the balance in various accounts. For example, the Cash account shows the amount of cash that is available to meet current obligations. Amounts due from customers can be found by examining Accounts Receivable, and amounts owed to creditors can be found by examining Accounts Payable.

The simple T-account form used in accounting textbooks is useful for illustration purposes. However, in practice, the account forms used in ledger are much more structured. A widely used form is shown below using assumed data from a cash account.

Three-Column Form of Account

	CASH			No. 101	
Date	Explanation	Ref.	Debit	Credit	Balance
2017					
June 1			25,000		25,000
2				8,000	17,000
3			4,200		21,200
9			7,500		28,700
17				11,700	17,000
20				250	16,750
30				7,300	9,450

This form is often called the three-column form of account because it has three money columns—debit, credit, and balance. The balance in the account is determined after each transaction. Note that the explanation space and reference columns are used to provide special information about the transaction.

2.7 Posting

The procedure of transferring journal entries to the ledger accounts is called posting. Posting involves the following steps.

(1) In the ledger, enter in the appropriate columns of the account(s) debited the date, journal page, and debit amount shown in the journal.

(2) In the reference column of the journal, write the account number to which the debit amount was posted.

(3) In the ledger, enter in the appropriate columns of the account(s) credited the data, journal page, and credit amount shown in the journal.

(4) In the reference column of the journal, write the account number to which the credit amount was posted.

Posting should be performed in chronological order. That is all the debits and credits of one journal entry should be posted before proceeding to the next journal entry. Postings should be made on a timely basis to ensure that the ledger is up to date.

The reference column **in the journal** serves several purposes. The numbers in this column indicate the entries that have been posted. After the last entry has been posted, this column should be scanned to see that all postings have been made.

The reference column **of a ledger** account indicates the journal page from which the transaction was posted. The explanation space of the ledger account is used infrequently because an explanation already appears in the journal. It generally is used only when detailed analysis of account activity is required.

> **HELPFUL HINT**
> How can one tell whether all postings have been completed?
> Answer: Scan the reference column of the journal to see whether there are any blanks opposite account titles. If there are no blanks, all postings have been made.

The number and type of accounts used differ for each enterprise. The number of accounts depends on the amount of detail desired by management. For example, the management of one company may want one account for all types of utility expense. Another may keep separate expense accounts for each type of utility, such as gas, electricity, and water. Similarly, a single proprietorship like **Softbyte** will have fewer accounts than a corporate giant like **Ford Motor Company**. Softbyte may be able to manage and report its activities in twenty to thirty accounts, while Ford requires thousands to keep track of its worldwide activities.

Most companies have a chart of account that lists the accounts and the account numbers that identify their location in the ledger. The numbering system used to identify the accounts usually starts with the balance sheet accounts and follows with the income statement accounts.

In this and the next two units, we will explain the accounting for the proprietorship Pioneer Advertising Agency (a service enterprise). Accounts 101~199 indicate asset accounts; 200~299 indicate liabilities; 301~350 indicate owner's equity accounts; 400~499, revenues; 601~799, expenses; 800~899, other revenues and 900~999, other expenses.

The chart of accounts for Pioneer Advertising Agency (C. R. Byrd, owner) is shown below.

CHART OF ACCOUNTS
PIONEER ADVERTISING AGENCY

Assets	Owner's Equity
101 Cash	301 C. R. Byrd, Capital
112 Accounts Receivable	306 C. R. Byrd, Drawing
126 Advertising Supplies	350 Income Summary
130 Prepaid Insurance	
157 Office Equipment	**Revenues**
158 Accumulated Depreciation—Office Equipment	400 Service Revenue
Liabilities	**Expenses**
200 Notes Payable	631 Advertising Supplies Expense
201 Accounts Payable	711 Depreciation Expense
209 Unearned Revenue	722 Insurance Expense
212 Salaries Payable	726 Salaries Expense
230 Interest Payable	729 Rent Expense
	905 Interest Expense

You will notice that there are gaps in the numbering system of the chart of accounts for Pioneer Advertising Agency. Gaps are left to permit the insertion of new accounts as needed during the life of the business.

2.8 • The Trial Balance

A trial balance is a list of accounts and their balances at a given time. Customarily, a trial balance is prepared at the end of an accounting period. The accounts are listed in the order in which they appear in the ledger; debit balances are listed in the left column and credit balances in the right column.

The primary purpose of a trial balance is to prove (check) that the debits equal the credits after posting. In other words, the sum of the debit account balances in the trial balance should equal the sum of the credit account balances. **If the debits and credits do not agree, the**

trial balance can be used to uncover errors in journalizing and posting. **In addition, it is useful in the preparation of financial statements.**

The steps for preparing a trial balance are:

(1) List the account titles and their balances.

(2) Total the debit and credit columns.

(3) Prove the equality of the two columns.

The trial balance prepared from Pioneer Advertising Agency's ledger is shown below.

PIONEER ADVERTISING AGENCY
Trial Balance
October 31, 2017

	Debit	Credit
Cash	$ 15,200	
Advertising Supplies	2,500	
Prepaid Insurance	600	
Office Equipment	5,000	
Notes Payable		$ 5,000
Accounts Payable		2,500
Unearned Revenue		1,200
C. R. Byrd, Capital		10,000
C. R. Byrd, Drawing	500	
Service Revenue		10,000
Salaries Expense	4,000	
Rent Expense	900	
	$ 28,700	$ 28,700

Note that the total debits ($ 28,700) equal the total credits ($ 28,700). Account numbers are sometimes shown to the left of the account titles in the trial balance.

A trial balance is a necessary checkpoint for uncovering certain types of errors before you proceed to other steps in the accounting process. For examples, if only the debit portion of a journal entry has been posted, the trial balance would bring this error to light.

2.8.1 Limitations of a Trail Balance

A trial balance does not guarantee freedom from recording errors, however. **It does not prove that all transactions have been recorded or that the ledger is correct.** Numerous errors may exist even though the trial balance columns agree. For example, the trial balance may balance even when (1) a transaction is not journalized, (2) a correct journal entry is not posted, (3) a journal entry is posted twice, (4) incorrect accounts are used in journalizing or posting, or (5) offsetting errors are made in recording the amount of a transaction. In other words, as long as equal debits and credits are posted, even to the wrong account or in the wrong amount, the total debits will equal the total credits.

2.8.2 Locating Errors

The procedure for preparing a trial balance is relatively simple. However, if the trial balance does not balance, locating an error in a manual system can be time-consuming, tedious, and frustrating. Errors generally result from mathematical mistakes, incorrect postings, or simply transcribing data incorrectly.

What do you do if you are faced with a trial balance that does not balance? First determine the amount of the difference between the two columns of the trial balance. After this amount is known, the following steps are often helpful:

(1) If the error is $1, $10, $100, $1,000, or $10,000, re-add the trial balance columns and re-compute the account balances.

(2) If the error is divisible by 2, scan the trial balance to see whether a balance equal to half the error has been entered in the wrong column.

(3) If the error is divisible by 9, retrace the account balances on the trial balance to see whether they are incorrectly copied from the ledger. For example, if a balance was $12 and it was listed as $21, a $9 has been made. Reversing the order of numbers is called a transposition error.

(4) If the error is not divisible by 2 or 9 (for example, $365), scan the ledger to see whether an account balance of $365 has been omitted from the trial balance, and scan the journal to see whether a $365 posting has been omitted.

2.8.3 Use of Dollar Signs

Note that dollar signs do not appear in the journals or ledgers. Dollar signs are usually used only in the trial balance and the financial statements. Generally, a dollar is shown only for the first item in the column and for the total of that column. A single line is placed under the column of figures to be added or subtracted; the total amount is double underlined to indicate the final sum.

Key Words and Expressions

1. account 账户
2. debit 借方；借记
3. credit 贷方；贷记
4. balance 余额
5. double-entry system 复式记账
6. journal 日记账
7. ledger 分类账
8. book 账簿
9. general journal 普通日记账
10. compound entry 复合分录
11. accounts payable 应付账款
12. posting 过账

13. chart of accounts 会计科目表
14. accounts receivable 应收账款
15. prepaid insurance 预付保险费
16. office equipment 办公设备
17. accumulate depreciation 累计折旧
18. notes payable 应付票据
19. unearned revenue 预收账款
20. service revenue 劳务收入
21. trial balance 试算平衡表

Exercises

Case 1

Presented below is the information related to Marx Real Estate Agency.

Oct. 1 Lynn Marx begins business as a real estate agent with a cash investment of $10,000.

2 Hires an administrative assistant.

3 Purchases office furniture for $1,900, on account.

6 Sells a house and lot for B. Rollins; bills B. Rollins $3,200 for realty services provided.

27 Pays $700 on the balance related to the transaction of October 3.

30 Pays the administrative assistant $1,500 in salary for October.

Instructions

Journalize the transactions.

Case 2

The accounts in the ledger of Tardy Delivery Service contain the following balances on July 31, 2002.

Accounts Receivable	$8,642	Prepaid Insurance	$1,968
Accounts Payable	8,396	Repair Expense	961
Cash	?	Service Revenue	10,610
Delivery Equipment	49,360	I. M. Tardy, Drawing	700
Gas and Oil Expense	758	I. M. Tardy, Capital	44,636
Insurance Expense	523	Salaries Expense	4,428
Notes Payable	21,450	Salaries Payable	815

Instructions

Prepare a trial balance with the accounts arranged as illustrated in the unit and fill in the missing amount for Cash.

Extended Reading

Filing of Documentation

Filing must be on shelving correctly labelled to enable quick, easy, and safe accessibility at all times. It is a waste of time and potentially a breach of occupational health and safety to simply heap the files into an inaccessible corner and hope they are never required.

(1) Source Documents

A source (or business) document is prepared at the time a business transaction actually takes place. On this document are recorded all relevant details concerning the transaction. The document provides evidence that the transaction has taken place. Business documents are the source of most entries in the accounting records.

• Invoice	A bill charging a customer for goods supplied or service provided on credit
• Credit Note	A document which allows a customer a reduction in the original amount charged for goods or services supplied on credit
• Cheque	An order to a bank to pay a sum of money to a specified person
• Receipt	A written acknowledgement of money received
• Bank Deposit Slip	A document prepared when depositing cash/cheques in a bank account
• Cash Sale Docket	A customer receipt prepared by a cash register or hand written for a cash sales transaction

(2) Filling of Payments

Purchases on credit will eventually need to be paid. They can be filed by sequential cheque number.

The purchase tax invoice, checked, authorised and approved should have attached to it.

The business copy of the authorised purchase order should show:

-the account to which the purchase is to be allocated in the financial

-the price and quantity required

-the date the purchase is required to be delivered to the business

-a signed delivery docket indicating the receipt of the quantity on the purchase order.

The number of the purchase tax invoice is listed on the cheque requisition summary, together with any other purchase tax invoices and attachments being paid to the same supplier. All are filled together under the sequential number that is unique to that payment.

Other cheque payments should also be filled with the authorised and approved payment documentation so that the cheque signatories can also check that all tax invoices are approved for payment before they actually sign the cheque for payment.

(3) Filling of Receipts

Business copies of the sales tax invoices are usually filed sequentially by their tax invoice number. A credit sale should eventually result in a cheque being received from the customer to whom the credit sale was made. The cheque will be accompanied by a remittance advice indicating the tax invoices being paid. If there is no remittance advice, one must be prepared internally, showing the total of the cheque and the details of what is probably being paid. It may be necessary to contact the customer to confirm which tax invoices are being paid. The duplicate of the bank deposit must be stamped by the bank and signed by a senior accounting officer when it comes back from the bank. It is filed with the remittance advices and any duplicate receipts where they are prepared by the business.

The remittance advice details need to be filed chronologically and agreed by adding tape to the total of the day's banking.

All receipts, remittance details and duplicate deposits are filed together in chronological order.

Unit 3
Adjusting the Accounts

Learning Objectives

After studying this unit, you should be able to:
1. Explain the accrual basis of accounting;
2. Explain why adjusting entries are needed;
3. Identify the major types of adjusting entries;
4. Prepare adjusting entries for prepayments;
5. Prepare adjusting entries for accruals;
6. Describe the nature and purpose of an adjusted trial balance.

3.1 Accrual-Basis VS. Cash-Basis Accounting

What you will learn in this unit is accrual-basis accounting. Under the accrual basis, transactions that change a company's financial statements are recorded **in the periods in which the events occur**. For example, using the accrual basis to determine net income means recognizing revenues when earned (rather than when the cash is received). It also means recognizing expenses when incurred (rather than when paid). Information presented on an accrual basis reveals relationships likely to be important in predicting future results. Under accrual accounting, revenues are recognized when services are performed, so trends in revenues are thus more meaningful for decision-making.

An alternative to the accrual basis is the cash basis. Under cash-basis accounting, revenue is recorded when cash is received, and an expense is recorded when cash is paid. The cash basis often leads to misleading financial statements. It fails to record revenue that has been earned but for which the cash has not been received. Also, expenses are not matched with earned revenues. **Cash-basis accounting is not in accordance with generally accepted accounting principles (GAAP).**

Most companies use accrual-basis accounting. Individuals and some small companies use cash-basis accounting. The cash basis is justified for small businesses because they often have few receivables and payables. Accountants are sometimes asked to convert cash-basis records to the accrual basis. As you might expect, extensive adjusting entries are required for this task.

Determining the amount of revenues and expenses to be reported in a given accounting period can be difficult. To help in this task, accounting have developed two principles as part of generally accepted accounting principles (GAAP): the revenue recognition principle and the matching principle.

The revenue recognition principle dictates that revenue be recognized in the accounting period in which it is earned. **In a service is performed, revenue is considered to be earned at the time the service is performed.** To illustrate, assume that a dry cleaning business cleans clothing on June 30 but customers do not claim and pay for their clothes until the first week of July. Under the revenue recognition principle, revenue is received at June 30. At June 30, the dry cleaner would report a receivable on its balance sheet and revenue in its income statement for the service performed.

Accountants follow the approach of "let expenses follow revenues". That is expense recognition. It is tied to revenue recognition. In the preceding example, this principle means that the salary expense incurred in performing the cleaning service on June 30 should be reported in the income statement for the same period in which the service revenue is recognized. The critical issue in expense recognition is when the expense makes its contribution to revenue. This may or may not be the same period in which the expense is paid. If the salary incurred on June 30 is not paid until July, the dry cleaner would report salaries payable on its June 30 balance sheet. The practice of expense recognition is referred to as the matching principle because it dictates that efforts (expense) be matched with accomplishments (revenues).

Once the economic life of a business has been divided into artificial time periods, the revenue recognition and matching principles can be applied. This one assumption and two principles thus provide guidelines as to when revenues and expenses should be reported. These relationships are shown below.

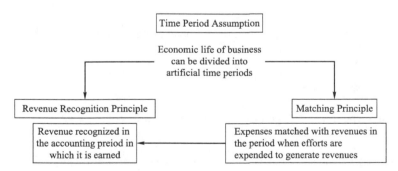

3.2 The Basics of Adjusting Entries

In order for revenues to be recorded in the period in which they are earned, and for expenses to be recognized in the period in which they are incurred, adjusting entries are made at the end of the accounting period. In short, **adjusting entries are needed to ensure that the revenue recognition and matching principles are followed.**

Adjusting entries make it possible to report on the balance sheet the appropriate assets, liabilities, and owner's equity at the statement date and to report on the income statement the proper net income (or loss) for the period. However, the trial balance—the first pulling together of the transaction data—may not contain up-to-date and complete date. This is true for the following reasons.

(1) Some events are not journalized daily because it is inexpedient to do so. Examples are the consumption of supplies and the earning of wages by employees.

(2) Some costs are not journalized during the accounting period because they expire with the passage of time rather than through recurring daily transactions. Examples are equipment deterioration, and rent and insurance.

(3) Some items many be unrecorded. An example is a utility service bill that will not be received until the next accounting period.

Adjusting entries are required every time financial statements are prepared. The starting point is an analysis of each account in the trial balance to determine whether it is complete and up-to-date. The analysis requires a thorough understanding of the company's operation and the interrelationship of accounts. Preparing adjusting entries is often an involved process. The company may need to make inventory counts of supplies and repair parts. It may need to prepare supporting schedules of insurance policies, rental agreements, and other contractual commitments. Adjusting are often prepared after the balance sheet date. However, the adjusting entries are dated as of balance sheet date.

3.3 Types of Adjusting Entries

Adjusting entries can be classified as either prepayments or accruals. Each of these classes has two subcategories.

3.3.1 Prepayments

(1) Prepaid Expenses Expenses paid in cash and recorded as assets before they are used or consumed.

(2) Unearned Revenues Cash received and recorded as liabilities before.

3.3.2 Accruals

(1) Accrued Revenues Revenues earned but not yet received in cash or recorded.

(2) Accrued Expenses Expenses incurred but not yet paid or recorded.

Specific examples and explanation of each type of adjustment are given on as the follows. Each example is based on the October 31 trial balance of Pioneer Advertising Agency.

PIONEER ADVERTISING AGENCY
Trial Balance
October 31, 2017

	Debit	Credit
Cash	$ 15,200	
Advertising Supplies	2,500	
Prepaid Insurance	600	
Office Equipment	5,000	
Notes Payable		$ 5,000
Accounts Payable		2,500
Unearned Revenue		1,200
C. R. Byrd, Capital		10,000
C. R. Byrd, Drawing	500	
Service Revenue		10,000
Salaries Expense	4,000	
Rent Expense	900	
	$ 28,700	$ 28,700

We assume that Pioneer Advertising uses an accounting period of one month. Thus, monthly adjusting entries will be made. The entries will be dated October 31.

3.4 • Adjusting Entries for Prepayments

As indicated earlier, prepayments are either prepaid expenses or unearned revenues. Adjusting entries for prepayments are required to record the portion of the prepayment that represents the **expense incurred or the revenue earned** in the current accounting period.

If an adjustment is needed for prepayments, the asset and liability are overstated and the related expense and revenue are understated before the adjustment. For example, in the trial balance, the balance in the asset Advertising Supplies shows only supplies purchased. This balance is overstated; a related expense Account, Advertising Supplies Expense, is understated because the cost of supplies used has not been recognized. Thus the adjusting entry for prepayments will **decrease a balance sheet account** (Advertising Supplies) and **increase an Income Statement account** (Advertising Supplies Expense). The effects of adjusting entries for prepayments are graphically depicted in the following illustration.

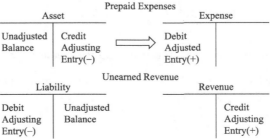

3.4.1　Prepaid Expenses

As stated before, expenses paid in cash and recorded as assets before they are used or consumed are called prepaid expenses. When a cost is prepaid, an asset account is debited to show the service or benefit that will be received in the future. Prepayments often occur in regard to insurance, supplies, advertising, and rent. In addition, prepayments are made when buildings and equipment are purchased.

Prepaid expenses expire either with the passage of time (e.g. rent and insurance) or through use and consumption (e.g. supplies). The expiration of these costs does not require daily journal entries, which would be unnecessary and impractical. Instead, it is customary to postpone recognizing cost expiration until financial statements are prepared. At each statement date, adjusting entries are made for two purposes: (1) to record the expenses that apply to the current accounting period, and (2) to show the unexpired costs in the asset accounts.

Prior to adjustment, assets are overstated and expenses are understated. Thus, the prepaid expense adjusting entry results in a debit (increase) to an expense account and a credit (decrease) to an asset account.

3.4.2　Supplies

Businesses use various types of supplies. For example, a CPA firm will have **office supplies** such as stationery, envelopes, and accounting paper. An advertising firm will have **advertising supplies** such as graph paper, video film, and poster paper. Supplies are generally debited to an asset account when they are acquired. In the course of operations, supplies are depleted, but recognition of supplies used is deferred until the adjustment process. At that point, a physical inventory (count) of supplies is taken. The difference between the balance in the Supplies (asset) account and the cost of supplies on hand represents the supplies used (expense) for the period.

Pioneer Advertising Agency purchased advertising supplies costing $2,500 on October 5. A debit (increase) was made to the asset Advertising Supplies. This account shows a balance of $2,500 in the October 31 trial balance. An inventory count at the close of business on October 31 reveals that $1,000 of supplies are still on hand. Thus, the cast of supplies used is $1,500 ($2,500 − $1,000), and the following adjusting entry is made.

Oct. 31	Advertising Supplies Expense	1,500	
	Advertising Supplies		1,500
	(To record supplies used)		

After the adjusting entry is posted, the two supplies accounts show:

Advertising Supplies				Advertising Supplies Expense		
10/5	2,500	10/31 Adj.	1,500	10/31 Adj.	1,500	
10/31 Bal.	1,000					

The asset account Advertising Supplies now shows a balance of $1,000 which is the cost of supplies on hand at the statement date. In addition, Advertising Supplies Expense shows a balance of $1,500, which equals the cost of supplies used in October. **If the adjusting entry is not made, October expenses will be understated and net income overstated by $1,500. Also, both assets and owner's equity will be overstated by $1,500 on the October 31 balance sheet.**

3.4.3 Insurance

Most companies have fire and theft insurance on merchandise and equipment, personal liability insurance for accidents suffered by customers, and automobile insurance on company cars and trucks. The cost of insurance protection is determined by the payment of insurance premiums. The minimum term of coverage is usually one year, but three-five-year terms are available and offer lower annual premiums. Insurance premiums normally are charged to the asset account Prepaid Insurance when paid. At the financial statement date, necessary to debit (increase) Insurance Expense and credit (decrease) Prepaid Insurance for the cost that has expired during the period.

On October 4, Pioneer Advertising Agency paid $600 for a one-year fire insurance policy. The effective date of coverage was October 1. The premium was charged to Prepaid Insurance when it was paid, and this account shows a balance of $600 in the October 31 trial balance. Analysis reveals that $50 ($600÷12) of insurance expires each month. Thus, the following adjusting entry is made.

Oct. 31 Insurance Expense   50
           Prepaid Insurance   50
         (To record insurance expired)

After the adjusting entry is posted, the accounts show:

Prepaid Insurance			Insurance Expense		
10/4	600	10/31 Adj. 50	10/31 Adj.	50	
10/31 Bal.	550				

The asset Prepaid Insurance shows a balance of $550. This amount represents the unexpired cost for the remaining eleven months of coverage. The $50 balance is Insurance Expense in equal to the insurance cost that has expired in October. **If this adjustment is not made, October expense will be understated by $50 and net income assets and income overstated by $50. Also, both assets and owner's equity will be overstated by $50 on October 31 balance sheet.**

3.4.4 Depreciation

A **business** enterprise typically owns productive facilities such as buildings, equipment, and vehicles. Because these assets provide service for a number of years, each is recorded as an asset, rather than an expense, in the year it is acquired. Such assets are recorded at cost, as required by the cost principle. The term of service is referred to as the **useful life.**

According to the matching principle, a portion of the cost of a long-lived asset should be reported as an expense during each period of the asset's useful life. **Depreciation** is the allocation of the cost of an asset to expense over its useful life in a rational and systematic manner.

Need for Depreciation Adjustment. From an accounting standpoint, acquiring productive facilities is viewed essentially as long-term prepayment for services. The need for periodic adjusting entries for depreciation is, therefore, the same as that for other prepaid expenses: to recognize the cost that has expired (expense) during the period and to report the unexpired cost (asset) at the end of the period.

At the time an asset is acquired, its useful life cannot be known with certainty. The asset may be useful for a longer or shorter time than expected, depending on such factors as actual use, deterioration due to the elements or obsolescence. Thus, you should recognize that **depreciation is an estimate** rather than a factual measurement of the cost that has expired. A common procedure in computing depreciation expense is to divide the cost of the asset by its useful life. For example, if cost is $10,000 and useful life is expired to be 10 years, annual depreciation is $1,000.

For Pioneer Adverting, depreciation on the office equipment is estimated to be $480 a year, or $40 per month. Accordingly, depreciation for October is recognized by the following adjusting entry.

Oct. 31 Depreciation Expense   40
            Accumulated Depreciation—Office Equipment   40
         (To record monthly depreciation)

The balance in the accumulated depreciation account will increase $40 each month. After journalizing and posting the adjusting entry at November 30, the balance will be $80; at December 31, $120; and so on.

Statement Presentation. Accumulated Depreciation—Office Equipment is a contra asset account. A contra asset account is one that is offset against an asset account on the balance sheet. This accumulated depreciation account appears just after Office Equipment on the balance sheet. Its normal balance is a credit. An alternative would be to credit (decrease) Office Equipment directly for the deprecation each month. But use of the contra account provides disclosure of **both the original** of the equipment **and the cost that has expired to date.** In the balance sheet, Accumulated Depreciation—Office Equipment is deducted from the related asset account as follows.

Office Equipment	$5,000	
Less: Accumulated Depreciation—Office Equipment	40	**$4,960**

The difference between the cost of any depreciable asset and its related accumulated depreciation is referred to as the **book value** of that asset. In the above illustration, the book value of the equipment at the balance sheet date is $4,960. You should realize that the book value is generally different from the market value (the price at witch the asset could be sold in the marketplace). The reason why the two are different is that depreciation is a means of cost allocation, not a matter of valuation.

Depreciation expense also identifies that portion of the asset's cost that has expired in October. As in the case of other prepaid adjustments, the omission of this adjusting entry would cause total assets, total owner's equity, and net income to be overstated and depreciation expense to be understated.

If the company owns additional equipment, such as delivery or store equipment, or if it has buildings, depreciation expense is recorded on each of those items. Related accumulated depreciation accounts are also established, such as: Accumulated Depreciation—Delivery Equipment; Accumulated Depreciation—Store Equipment; and Accumulated Depreciation—Buildings.

3.5　Adjusting Entries for Accruals

The second category of adjusting entries is **accruals**. Adjusting entries for accruals are required to record revenue earned and expense incurred in the current accounting period that have not been recognized through daily entries.

An accrual adjustment is needed when various accounts are understated: the revenue account and the related asset account, and/or the expense account and the related liability account. Thus, the adjusting entry for accruals will **increase both a balance sheet and an income statement account.** Adjusting entries for accruals are graphically depicted in the following Illustration.

ADJUSTING ENTRIES
Accrued Revenues

Asset	Revenue
Debit Adjusting Entry (+)	Credit Adjusting Entry (+)

Accrued Expense

Expense		Liability
Debit Adjusting Entry (+)		Credit Adjusting Entry (+)

3.5.1 Accrued Revenues

As explained on Trial Balance of **Pioneer Advertising Agency** on October 31, 2017, revenues earned but not yet received in cash or recorded at the statement date are accrued revenues. Accrued revenues may accumulate (accrue) with the passing of time, as in the case of interest revenue and rent revenue. Or they may result from services that have been performed but neither billed nor collected, as in the case of commissions and fees. The former are unrecorded because the earning of interest and rent does not involve daily transactions. The latter may be unrecorded because only a portion of the total service has been provided.

An adjusting entry is required for two purposes: (1) to show the receivable that exists at the balance sheet date, and (2) to record the revenue that has been earned during the period. Prior to adjustment both assets and revenues are understated. Thus, **an adjusting entry for accrued revenues results in a debit (increase) to an asset account and a credit (increase) to a revenue account.**

In October Pioneer Advertising Agency earned $200 for advertising services that were not billed to clients before October 31. Because these services have not been billed, they have not been recorded. The following adjusting entry is made.

Oct. 31	Accounts Receivable	200	
	Service Revenue		200
	(To record revenue for services provided)		

After the adjusting entry is posted, the accounts show:

Accounts Receivable		**Service Revenue**	
10/31 Adj. 200		10/31	10,000
		31	400
		31 Adj.	200
		10/31 Bal.	10,600

The asset Accounts Receivable shows that $200 is owed by clients at the balance sheet date. The balance of $10,600 in Service Revenue represents the total revenue earned during the month ($10,000+$400+$200). **If the adjusting entry is not made, the following will** all be understated: assets and owner's equity on the balance sheet, and revenues and net income on the income statement.

In the next accounting period, the clients will be billed. The entry to record the billing should recognize that a portion has already been recorded in the previous month's adjusting entry. To illustrate, assume that bills totaling $3,000 are mailed to clients on November 10. Of this amount, $200 represents revenue earned in October and is recorded as Service Revenue in the October 31 adjusting entry. The remaining $2,800 represents revenue earned in November. Thus, the following entry is made.

Nov. 10	Accounts Receivable	2,800	
	Service Revenue		2,800
	(To record revenue for services provided)		

This entry records services revenue between November 1 and November 10. The subsequent collection of revenue from clients (including the $200 earned in October) will be recorded with a debit (increase) to Cash and a credit (decrease) to Accounts Receivable.

3.5.2 Accrued Expenses

As indicated on Trial Balance of Pioneer Advertising Agency on October 31, 2002, expenses incurred but not yet paid or recorded at the statement date are called accrued expenses. Interest, rent, taxes, and salaries can be accrued expenses. Accrued expenses result from the same causes as accrued revenues. In fact, an accrued expense on books of one company is an accrued revenue to another company. For example, the $200 accrual of fees by Pioneer is an accrued expense to the client that received the service.

Adjustments for accrued expenses are needed for two purposes: (1) to record the obligations that exist at the balance sheet date, and (2) to recognize the expenses that apply to the current accounting period. Prior to adjustment, both liabilities and expenses are understated. Thus, the adjusting entry for accrued expenses results in a debit (increase) to an expense account and a credit (increase) to a liability account.

3.5.3 Accrued Interest

Pioneer Advertising Agency signed a $5,000, 3-month note payable on October 1. The note requires interest at an annual rate of 12%. (1) face value of the note, (2) the interest rate, which is always expressed as an annual rate, and (3) the length of time the note is outstanding. In this instance, the total interest due on the $5,000 note at its due date 3 months hence is $150 ($5,000 × 12% × 3/12), or $50 for one month. The formula for computing interest and its application to Pioneer Advertising Agency for the month of October 2 are shown below. Note that the time period is expressed as a fraction of a year.

Face Value of Note		Annual Interest		Time in Terms of One Year		Interest
	×		×		=	
$5000	×	2%	×	1/2	=	$50

The accrued expense adjusting entry at October 31 is:

Oct. 31	Interest Expense	50	
	Interest Payable		50
	(To record interest on notes payable)		

After this adjusting entry is posted, the accounts show:

Interest Expense		Interest payable	
10/30 Adj. 50		10/30 Adj. 50	

Interest Expense shows the interest charges for the month. The amount of interest owed at the statement date is shown in Interest Payable. It will not be paid until the note comes due at the end of 3 months. The Interest Payable account is used instead of crediting (increasing) Notes payable. **If this adjusting entry is not made, liabilities and interest expense will be understated, and net income and owner's equity will be overstated.**

3.5.4 Accrued Salaries

Some types of expenses are paid for after the services have been performed. Examples are employee salaries and commissions. At Pioneer Advertising, salaries were last paid on October 26; the next payday is November 9. As shown in the calendar, three working days remain in October (October 29-31)

October

S	M	Tu	W	Th	F	S
	1	2	3	4	5	6
7	8	9	10	11	12	13
14	(15)	16	17	18	19	20
21	22	23	24	25	(26)	27
28	29	30	31			

Start of pay period → 14, (15)

Adjustment period: 29-31
Payday: 26

November

S	M	Tu	W	Th	F	S
					1	2	3
4	5	6	7	8	(9)	10
11	12	13	14	15	16	17
18	19	20	21	22	23	24
25	26	27	28	29	30	

Payday: 9

At October 31, the salaries for the last there days of the month represent an accrued expense and a related liability. The employees receive total salaries of $2,000 for a five-day work week, or $400 per day. Thus, accrued salaries at October 31 are $1,200 ($400× 3). The adjusting entry is:

Oct. 31	Salaries Expense	1,200	
	Salaries Payable		1,200
	(To record accrued salaries)		

After this adjusting entry is posted, the accounts show:

Salaries Expense			Salaries Payable	
10/26	4,000			
10/31 Adj.	1,200		10/31 Adj.	1,200
10/31 Bal.	5,200			

After this adjustment, the balance in Salaries Expense of $5,200 (13 days × $400) is the actual salary expense for October. (The employees started work on October 15.) The balance in Salaries Payable of $1,200 is the amount of the liability for salaries owed as of October 31. **If the $1,200 adjustment for salaries is not recorded, Pioneer's expenses will be understated $1,200, and its liabilities will be understated $1,200.**

At Pioneer Advertising, salaries are payable every two weeks. The next payday is November 9, when total salaries of $4,000 will again be paid. The payment will consist of $1,200 of salaries payable at October 31 plus $2,800 of salaries expense for November (seven working days as shown in the November calendar × $400). Therefore, the following entry is made on November 9.

Nov. 9	Salaries Payable	1,200	
	Salaries Expense	2,800	
	Cash		4,000
	(To record accrued November 9 payroll)		

This entry does two things: (1) It eliminates the liability for Salaries Payable that was recorded in the October 31 adjusting entry. (2) It records the proper amount of Salaries Expense for the period between November 1 and November 9.

3.5.5 Summary of Basic Relationships

The four basic types of adjusting entries are summarized in **the following form.** Take some to study and analyze the adjusting entries shown in the summary. Be sure to note that **each adjusting entry affects one balance sheet account and one income statement account.**

Type of Adjustment	Reason for Adjustment	Accounts before Adjustment	Adjusting Entry
1. Prepaid expenses	Prepaid expenses originally recorded in asset accounts have been used	Assets overstated Expenses understated	Dr. Expenses Cr. Assets
2. Unearned revenues	Unearned revenues initially recorded in liability accounts have been earned	Liabilities overstated Revenues understated	Dr. Liabilities Cr. Revenues
3. Accrued revenues	Revenues have been earned but not yet received in cash or recorded	Assets overstated Revenues understated	Dr. Assets Cr. Revenues
4. Accrued expenses	Expenses have been incurred but not yet paid in cash or recorded	Expenses overstated Liabilities understated	Dr. Expenses Cr. Liabilities

The journalizing and posting of adjusting entries for Pioneer Advertising Agency on October 31 are shown in **the following journal.** All adjustments are identified in the ledger by the reference J2 because they have been journalized on page 2 of the general journal. A center caption entitled "Adjusting Entries" may be inserted between the lost transaction entry and the first adjusting entry to identify these entries.

GENERAL JOURNAL J2

Date	Accounting Titles and Explanation	Ref.	Debit	Credit
2017	Adjusting Entries			
Oct. 31	Advertising Supplies Expense	631	1,500	
	Advertising Supplies	126		1,500
	(To record Supplies used)			
31	Insurance Expense	722	50	
	Prepaid Insurance	130		50
	(To record Insurance expired)			
31	Depreciation Expense	711	40	
	Accumulated Depreciation—Office Equipment	158		40
	(To record monthly depreciation)			
31	Unearned Revenue	209	400	
	Service Revenue	400		400
	(To record revenue for service provided)			
31	Accounts Receivable	112	200	
	Service Revenue	400		200
	(To record revenue for service provided)			
31	Interest Expense	905	50	
	Interest Payable	230		50
	(To record interest on notes payable)			
31	Salaries Expense	726	1,200	
	Salaries Payable	212		1,200
	(To record interest on notes payable)			

Cash No. 101

Date	Explanation	Ref.	Debit	Credit	Balance
2017					
Oct. 1		J1	10,000		10,000
2		J1	1,200		11,200
3		J1		900	10,300
4		J1		600	9,700
20		J1		500	9,200
26		J1		4,000	5,200
31		J1	10,000		15,200

Accounts Receivable No. 112

Date	Explanation	Ref.	Debit	Credit	Balance
2017					
Oct. 31	Adj. entry	J2	200		200

Advertising Supplies　　　　　　　　　　　　　　　　　　　　　　　　　　　　No. 126

Date	Explanation	Ref.	Debit	Credit	Balance
2017 Oct. 5		J1	2,500		2,500
	Adj. entry	J2		1,500	1,000

Prepaid Insurance　　　　　　　　　　　　　　　　　　　　　　　　　　　　　No. 130

Date	Explanation	Ref.	Debit	Credit	Balance
2017 Oct. 4		J1	600		600
31	Adj. entry	J2		50	550

Office Equipment　　　　　　　　　　　　　　　　　　　　　　　　　　　　　No. 157

Date	Explanation	Ref.	Debit	Credit	Balance
2017 Oct. 1		J1	5,000		5,000

Accumulated Depreciation—Office Equipment　　　　　　　　　　　　　　　　No. 158

Date	Explanation	Ref.	Debit	Credit	Balance
2017 Oct. 31	Adj. entry	J2	40		40

Notes Payable　　　　　　　　　　　　　　　　　　　　　　　　　　　　　　No. 200

Date	Explanation	Ref.	Debit	Credit	Balance
2017 Oct. 1		J1	5,000		5,000

Accounts Payable　　　　　　　　　　　　　　　　　　　　　　　　　　　　　No. 201

Date	Explanation	Ref.	Debit	Credit	Balance
2017 Oct. 5		J1	2,500		2,500

Unearned Revenue　　　　　　　　　　　　　　　　　　　　　　　　　　　　No. 209

Date	Explanation	Ref.	Debit	Credit	Balance
2017 Oct. 2		J1		1,200	
31	Adj. entry	J2	400		800

Salaries Payable   No. 212

Date		Explanation	Ref.	Debit	Credit	Balance
2017						
Oct.	31	Adj. entry	J2		1,200	1,200

Interest Payable   No. 230

Date		Explanation	Ref.	Debit	Credit	Balance
2017						
Oct.	31	Adj. entry	J2		50	50

C. R. Byrd, Capital   No. 301

Date		Explanation	Ref.	Debit	Credit	Balance
2017						
Oct.	1		J1		10,000	10,000

C. R. Byrd, Drawing   No. 306

Date		Explanation	Ref.	Debit	Credit	Balance
2017						
Oct.	1		J1		500	500

Service Revenue   No. 400

Date		Explanation	Ref.	Debit	Credit	Balance
2017						
Oct.	31		J1		10,000	10,000
		Adj. entry	J2		400	10,400
		Adj. entry	J2		200	10,600

Advertising Supplies Expense   No. 631

Date		Explanation	Ref.	Debit	Credit	Balance
2017						
Oct.	31	Adj. entry	J2	1,500		1,500

Depreciation Expense   No. 711

Date		Explanation	Ref.	Debit	Credit	Balance
2017						
Oct.	31	Adj. entry	J2	40		40

Insurance Expense No. 722

Date	Explanation	Ref.	Debit	Credit	Balance
2017					
Oct. 31	Adj. entry	J2	50		50

Salaries Expense No. 726

Date	Explanation	Ref.	Debit	Credit	Balance
2017					
Oct. 26		J1	4,000		4,000
31	Adj. entry	J2	1,200		5,200

Rent Expense No. 729

Date	Explanation	Ref.	Debit	Credit	Balance
2017					
Oct. 3		J1	900		900

Interest Expense No. 905

Date	Explanation	Ref.	Debit	Credit	Balance
2017					
Oct. 31	Adj. entry	J1	50		50

3.6 The Adjusted Trial Balance

After all adjusting entries have been journalized and posted, another trial balance is prepared from the ledger accounts. This is called an adjusted trial balance. Its purpose is to prove the equality of the total debit balances and the total credit balances in the ledger after all adjustments have been made. The accounts in the adjusted trial balance contain all data needed for the preparation of financial statements.

The adjusted trial balance for Pioneer Advertising Agency is presented below.

PIONEER ADVERTISING AGENCY
Adjusted Trial Balance
October 31, 2017

	Dr.	Cr.
Cash	$15,200	
Accounts Receivable	200	
Advertising Supplies	1,000	
Prepaid Insurance	550	
Office Equipment	5,000	
Accumulated Depreciation—Office Equipment		$40
Notes Payable		5,000
Accounts Payable		2,500
Unearned Revenue		800
Salaries Payable		1,200
Interest Payable		50
C. R. Byrd, Capital		10,000
C. R. Byrd, Drawing	500	
Service Revenue		10,600
Salaries Expense	5,200	
Advertising Supplies Expense	1,500	
Rent Expense	900	
Insurance Expense	50	
Interest Expense	50	
Depreciation Expense	40	
Total	$30,190	$30,190

Key Words and Expressions

1. adjust 调整
2. accrual-basis accounting 权责发生制
3. cash-basis accounting 现金收付制
4. generally accepted accounting principles 公认会计原则
5. revenue recognition principle 收入确认原则
6. matching principle 配比原则
7. adjusting entry 调整分录
8. office supplies 办公用品
9. insurance 保险
10. depreciation 折旧

11. useful life 使用年限
12. allocation 分配
13. book value 账面价值
14. face value 面值
15. interest 利息
16. annual interest 年利率

Exercises

Case 1

The ledger of Easy Rent Agency on March of the current year includes the following selected accounts before adjusting entries have been prepared.

	Debit	Credit
Prepaid Insurance	$ 3,600	
Supplies	2,800	
Equipment	25,000	
Accumulated Depreciation—Equipment		$ 8,400
Notes payable		20,000
Unearned Rent		9,900
Rent Revenue		60,000
Interest Expense	-0-	
Wage Expense	14,000	

An analysis of the accounts shows the following.

(1) The equipment depreciates $ 250 per month.

(2) One-third of the unearned rent was earned during the quarter.

(3) Interest of $ 500 is accrued on the notes payable.

(4) Supplies on hand total $ 650.

(5) Insurance expires at the rate of $ 300 per month.

Instructions

Prepare the adjusting entries at March 31, assuming that adjusting entries are made quarterly. Additional accounts are: Depreciation Expense, Insurance Expense, Interest Payable, and Supplies Expense.

Case 2

Karen Tong, D. D. S. , opened a dental practice on January 1, 2012. During the first month of operations the following transactions occurred.

(1) Performed services for patients who had dental plan insurance. At January 31, $ 875 of such services was earned but not yet billed to the insurance companies.

(2) Utility expenses incurred but not paid prior to January 31 totaled $ 520.

(3) Purchased dental equipment on January 1 for $ 80,000, paying $ 20,000 in cash

and signing a $60,000, 3-year note payable. The equipment depreciates $400 per month. Interest is $500 per month.

(4) Purchased a one-year malpractice insurance policy on January 1 for $22,000.

(5) Purchased $1,600 of dental supplies. On January 31, determined that $700 of supplies were on hand.

Instructions

Prepare the adjusting entries on January 31. Account titles are: Accumulated Depreciation—Dental Equipment, Depreciation Expense, Service Revenue, Accounts Receivable, Insurance Expense, Interest Expense, Interest Payable, Prepaid Insurance, Supplies Expense, Utilities Expense, and Utilities Payable.

Case 3

The income statement of Weller Co. for the month of July shows net income of $1,400 based on Service Revenue $5,500, Wages Expense $2,300, Supplies Expense $1,200, and Utilities Expense $600. In reviewing the statement, you discover the following.

(1) Insurance expired during July of $400 was omitted.

(2) Supplies expense includes $500 of supplies that are still on hand at July 31.

(3) Depreciation on equipment of $150 was omitted.

(4) Accrued but unpaid wages at July 31 of $300 were not included.

(5) Services provided but unrecorded totaled $1,100.

Instructions

Prepare a correct income statement for July.

Extended Reading

Accounting Standards

The major professional accounting bodies in Australia, the Australian Society of Accountants and the Institute of Chartered Accountants in Australia, have jointly established the Australian Accounting Research Foundation (AARF) to conduct research into, and after due consultation to issue standards on, matters affecting the practice of accounting and auditing. It has established a number of boards, including the Accounting Standards Board, the Auditing Standards Board and the Public Sector Accounting Standards Board.

The Accounting Standards Review Board (ASRB) was established by the Commonwealth government in 1984 to review accounting standards and if thought fit, approve them. Approved accounting standards have legislative backing under the Companies Code, and therefore must be observed. At this stage not all of the standards produced by the AARF have been approved by the ASRB.

In September 1988, the roles of the AARF and the ASRB were merged, and the ASRB now has the role of initiating, as well as issuing *approved accounting standards*. This has taken the power of setting standards away from the professional bodies.

The Accounting Standards are designed to improve the quality and uniformity of financial reporting in Australia.

Accountants and prospective accountants must be aware that the approved Accounting Standards exist, and where to find details of them at any time. They should be aware of the contents of these Standards in general terms, so that they would quickly recognize when they are working in an area covered by a Standard, and look up the details and follow them.

Up-to-date Accounting Standards should be found in any professional accountant's handbook. These handbooks are updated regularly by the respective accounting body. The Standards may also be acquired on application to either the Australian Society of Accountants or the Institute of Chartered Accountants in Australia.

Unit 4
Completion of the Accounting Cycle

Learning Objectives ▶▶

After studying this unit, you should be able to:
1. Explain the process of closing the books;
2. Describe the content and purpose of a post-closing trial balance;
3. Explain the approaches to preparing correcting entries;
4. Identify the sections of a classified balance sheet.

In this unit we will explain the role of the work sheet in accounting as well as the remaining steps in the accounting cycle, most especially, the closing process, again using Pioneer Advertising Agency as an example. Then we will consider (1) correcting entries and (2) classified balance sheets. The content and organization of Unit 4 are as follows.

```
                    COMPLETION OF THE
                    ACCOUNTING CYCLE
```

Using a Work Sheet	Closing the Books	Summary of Accounting Cycle	Classified Balance Sheet
● Steps in preparation ● Preparing financial statements ● Preparing adjusting	● Preparing closing entries ● Posting closing entries ● Preparing a post-closing in a balance	● Reversing entries—an optional step ● Correcting entries—an avoidable step	● Standard classifications ● Balance sheet illustration

At the end of the accounting period, the accounts are made ready for the next period. This is called closing the books. In closing the books, it is necessary to distinguish between temporary and permanent accounts. Temporary or nominal accounts relate only to a given accounting period. They include all income statement accounts and owner's drawing. All temporary accounts are closed. In contrast, permanent or real accounts relate to one or more future accounting periods. They consist of all balance sheet accounts, including owner's capital. Permanent accounts are not closed. Instead, their balances are carried forward into the next accounting period. The following illustration identifies the accounts in each category.

TEMPORARY (NOMINAL)	PERMANENT (REAL)
These accounts are closed	These accounts are not closed
All revenue accounts	**All asset accounts**
All expense accounts	**All liability accounts**
Owner's drawing accounts	**Owner's capital account**

4.1　Preparing Closing Entries

At the end of the accounting period, the temporary account balances are transferred to the permanent owner's equity account, owner's capital, through the preparation of closing entries. Closing entries formally recognize in the ledger the transfer of net income (or net loss) and owner's drawing to owner's capital. The results of these entries are shown in the owner's equity statement. **These entries also produce a zero balance in each temporary account. These accounts are then ready to accumulate data in the next accounting period separate from the data of prior periods.** Permanent accounts are not closed.

Journalizing and posting closing entries is a required step in the accounting cycle. This step is performed after financial statements have been prepared. In contrast to the steps in the cycle that you have already studied, closing entries are generally journalized and posted **only at the end of a company's annual accounting period.** This practice facilitates the preparation of annual financial statements because all temporary accounts will contain data for the entire year.

In preparing closing entries, each income statement account could be closed directly to owner's capital. However, to do so would result in excessive detail in the permanent owner's capital account. Instead, the revenue and expense accounts are closed to another temporary account, Income Summary; only the net income or net loss is transferred from this account to owner's capital.

4.1.1　Closing Entries are Journalized in the General Journal

A center caption entitled Closing Entries, inserted in the journal between the last adjusted entry and the first closing entry, identifies these entries. Then the closing entries are posted to the ledger accounts.

Closing entries may be prepared directly from the adjusted balances in the ledger, from the income statement and balance sheet columns of the work sheet, or from the income and owner's equity statements. Separate closing entries could be prepared for each nominal account, but the following four entries accomplish the desired result more efficiently:

(1) Debit each revenue account for its balance, and credit Income Summary for total revenues.

(2) Debit Income Summary for total expenses, and credit each expense account for its balance.

(3) Debit Income Summary and credit Owner's Capital for the amount of net income.

(4) Debit Owner's Capital for the balance in the Owner's Drawing account, and credit Owner's Drawing for the same amount.

4.1.2 Closing Entries Illustrated

In practice, closing entries are generally prepared only at the end of the annual accounting period. However, to illustrate the journalizing and posting of closing entries, we will assume that Pioneer Advertising Agency closes its books monthly. The closing entries at October 31 are shown below.

GENERAL JOURNAL

Date	Accounting Titles and Explanation	Ref.	Debit	Credit
2017	Closing Entries (1)			
Oct. 31	Service Revenue	400	10,600	
	Income Summary	350		10,600
	(To close revenue account)(2)			
31	Income Summary	350	7,740	
	Advertising Supplies Expense	631		1,500
	Depreciation Expense	711		40
	Insurance Expense	722		50
	Salaries Expense	726		5,200
	Rent Expense	729		900
	Interest Expense	905		50
	(To close expense accounts)(3)			
31	Income Summary	350	2,860	
	C. R. Byrd, Capital	301		2,860
	(To close net income to capital)(4)			
31	C. R. Byrd, Capital	301	500	
	C. R. Byrd, Drawing	306		500
	(To close drawings to capital)			

Note that the amounts for Income Summary in entries (1) and (2) are the totals of the income statement credit and debit columns, respectively, in the work sheet.

A couple of cautions in preparing closing entries: (1) Avoid unintentionally doubling the revenue and expense balances rather than zeroing them. (2) Do not close owner's drawing through the Income Summary account. Owner's Drawing is not an expense, and it is not a factor in determining net income.

4.1.3 Posting Closing Entries

As part of the closing process, the temporary accounts (revenues, expenses, and owner's drawing) in T-account form are totaled, balanced, and double-ruled as shown below. The permanent accounts (assets, liabilities, and owner's capital) are not closed: A single rule is drawn beneath the current period entries, and the account balance carried forward to the next period is entered below the single rule. (For example, see C. R. Byrd, Capital)

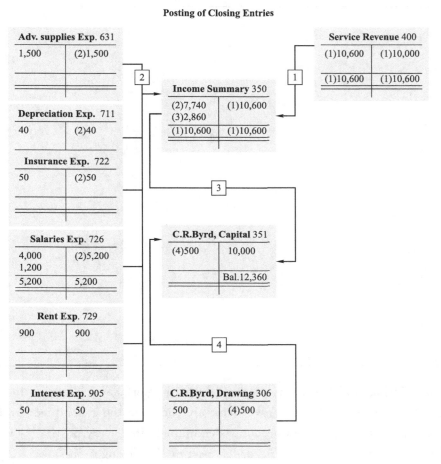

Posting of Closing Entries

4.2 Preparing Post-closing Trial Balance

After all closing entries have been journalized and posted, another trial balance, called a post-closing trial balance, is prepared from the ledger. The post-closing trial balance lists permanent accounts and their balances after closing entries have been journalized and posted. **The purpose of this trial balance is to prove the equality of the permanent account balances that are carried forward into the next accounting period.** Since all temporary accounts will have zero balances, **the post-closing trial balance will contain only permanent-balance sheet-accounts.**

The procedure for preparing a post-closing trial balance again consists entirely of listing the accounts and their balances. The post-closing trial balance for Pioneer Advertising Agency is shown below.

PIONEER ADVERTISING AGENCY
Post-closing Trial Balance
October 31, 2017

	Dr.	Cr.
Cash	$15,200	
Accounts Receivable	200	
Advertising Supplies	1,000	
Prepaid Insurance	550	
Office Equipment	5,000	
Accumulated Depreciation—Office Equipment		$40
Notes Payable		5,000
Accounts Payable		2,500
Unearned Revenue		800
Salaries Payable		1,200
Interest Payable		50
C. R. Byrd, Capital		12,360
Total	$21,950	$21,950

The post-closing trial balance is prepared from the permanent accounts in the ledger. The permanent accounts of Pioneer Advertising are shown in the general ledger. Remember that the balance of each permanent account is computed after every posting. Therefore, no additional work on these accounts is needed as part of the closing process.

A post-closing trial balance provides evidence that the journalizing and posting of closing entries have been properly completed. It also shows that the accounting equation is in balance at the end of the accounting period. However, like the trial balance, it does not prove that all transactions have been recorded or that the ledger is correct. For example, the post-closing trial balance will balance if a transaction is not journalized and posted or if a transaction is journalized and posted twice.

The remaining accounts in the general ledger are temporary accounts. After the closing entries are correctly posted, each temporary account has a zero balance. These accounts are double-ruled to finalize the closing process.

(Permanent Accounts only)

GENERAL LEDGER

Cash   No. 101

Date	Explanation	Ref.	Debit	Credit	Balance
2017					
Oct. 1		J1	10,000		10,000
2		J1	1,200		11,200
3		J1		900	10,300
4		J1		600	9,700
20		J1		500	9,200
26		J1		4,000	5,200
31		J1	10,000		15,200

Accounts Receivable   No. 112

Date	Explanation	Ref.	Debit	Credit	Balance
2017					
Oct. 31		J2	200		200

Advertising Supplies   No. 126

Date	Explanation	Ref.	Debit	Credit	Balance
2017					
Oct. 5		J1	2,500		2,500
		J2		1,500	1,000

Prepaid Insurance   No. 130

Date	Explanation	Ref.	Debit	Credit	Balance
2017					
Oct. 4		J1	600		600
31		J2		50	550

Office Equipment   No. 157

Date	Explanation	Ref.	Debit	Credit	Balance
2017					
Oct. 4		J1	5,000		5,000

Accounts Payable   No. 201

Date	Explanation	Ref.	Debit	Credit	Balance
2017					
Oct. 5		J1		2,500	2,500

Unearned Revenue   No. 209

Date	Explanation	Ref.	Debit	Credit	Balance
2017					
Oct. 2		J1		1,200	1,200
31		J2	400		800

Salaries Payable   No. 212

Date	Explanation	Ref.	Debit	Credit	Balance
2017					
Oct. 31	Adj. entry	J2		1,200	1,200

Interest Payable   No. 212

Date	Explanation	Ref.	Debit	Credit	Balance
2017					
Oct. 31	Adj. entry	J2		50	50

C. R. Byrd, Capital   No. 301

Date	Explanation	Ref.	Debit	Credit	Balance
2017					
Oct. 1		J1	10,000		10,000
2		J1	1,200		11,200
3		J1		900	10,300

NOTE: The permanent accounts for Pioneer Adverting Agency are shown here; the temporary accounts are shown in the next page. Both permanent and temporary accounts are part of the general ledger. They are segregated here to aid in learning.

Accumulated Depreciation—Office Equipment No. 158

Date	Explanation	Ref.	Debit	Credit	Balance
2017					
Oct. 31		J2		40	40

Notes Payable No. 200

Date	Explanation	Ref.	Debit	Credit	Balance
2017					
Oct. 31		J2		40	40

(Temporary Accounts only)

GENERAL LEDGER

C. R. Drawing No. 306

Date	Explanation	Ref.	Debit	Credit	Balance
2017					
Oct. 20		J1	500		500
		J3		500	0

Insurance Expense No. 722

Date	Explanation	Ref.	Debit	Credit	Balance
2017					
Oct. 31	Adj. entry	J2	50		50
31	Closing entry	J3		50	0

Income Summary No. 350

Date	Explanation	Ref.	Debit	Credit	Balance
2017					
Oct. 31		J3		10,600	10,600
31		J3	7,740		2,860
31		J3	2,860		0

Salaries Expense No. 726

Date	Explanation	Ref.	Debit	Credit	Balance
2017					
Oct. 20		J1	4,000		4,000
31	Adj. entry	J2	1,200		5,200
	Closing entry	J3		5,200	0

Service Revenue No. 400

Date	Explanation	Ref.	Debit	Credit	Balance
2017					
Oct. 31		J1		10,000	10,000
31	Adj. entry	J2		400	10,400
31	Adj. entry	J2		200	10,600
31	Closing entry	J3	10,600		0

Rent Expense No. 729

Date	Explanation	Ref.	Debit	Credit	Balance
2017					
Oct. 3		J1	900		900
31	Closing entry	J3		900	0

Advertising Supplies Expense No. 631

Date	Explanation	Ref.	Debit	Credit	Balance
2017					
Oct. 31	Adj. entry	J2	1,500		1,500
	Closing entry	J3		1,500	0

Interest Expense No. 905

Date	Explanation	Ref.	Debit	Credit	Balance
2017					
Oct. 31		J2	50		50
31	Closing entry	J3		50	0

Depreciation Expense No. 711

Date	Explanation	Ref.	Debit	Credit	Balance
2017					
Oct. 31	Adj. entry	J2	40		40
	Closing entry	J3		40	0

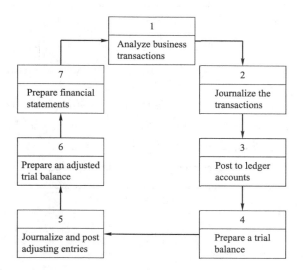

Optional steps: If a work sheet is prepared, steps, 4,5 and 6 are incorporated in work sheet.

4.3 Correcting Entries—an Avoidable Step

Unfortunately, errors may occur in the recording process. Errors should be corrected as soon as they are discovered by journalizing and posting correcting entries. If the accounting records are free of errors, no correcting entries are necessary.

You should recognize several difference between correcting entries and adjusting entries. First, adjusting entries are an integral part of the accounting cycle. Correcting entries, on the other hand, are unnecessary if the records are free of errors. Second, adjustments are journalized and posted only at the end of an accounting period. In contrast, correcting entries are made wherever an error is discovered. Finally, adjusting entries always affect at least one balance sheet account and one income statement account. In contrast, correcting entries may involve any combination of accounts in need of correction. Correcting entries must be posted before closing entries.

To determine the correcting entries, it is useful to compare the incorrect entry with the correct entry. Doing so helps identify the accounts and amounts that should and should not be corrected. After comparison, a correcting entry is made to correct the accounts. This approach is illustrated in the following two cases:

Case 1

On May 10, a $50 cash collection on account from a customer is journalized and posted as a debit to Cash and a credit to Service Revenue $50. The error is discovered on May 20, when the customer pays the remaining balance in full.

Incorrect Entry (May 10)		Correct Entry (May 10)	
Cash	50	Cash	50
Service Revenue	50	Accounts Receivable	50

A comparison of the incorrect entry with the correct entry reveals that the debit to Cash $50 is correct. However the $50 credit to Service Revenue should have been credited to Accounts Receivable. As a result, both Service Revenue and Accounts Receivable are overstated in the ledger. The following correcting entry is required.

Correct Entry (May 20)	
Service Revenue	50
Accounts Receivable	50

A	=	L	+	OE
−50				−50

Case 2

On May 18, office equipment costing $450 is purchased on account. The transaction is journalized and posted as a debit to Delivery Equipment $45 and a credit to Accounts Payable $45. The error is discovered on June 3, when the customer pays the remaining balance.

Incorrect Entry (May 18)		Correct Entry (May 18)	
Delivery Equipment	45	Office Equipment	450
Accounts Payable	45	Accounts Payable	450

A comparison of the two entries shows that three accounts are incorrect. Delivery Equipment is overstated $45; Office Equipment is understated $450; and Accounts Payable is understated $405. The correcting entry is:

Correct Entry (June 3)	
Office Equipment	450
Accounts Payable	405
Delivery Equipment	45

A	=	L	+	OE
+450				
−45		+405		

In stead of preparing a correcting entry, **it is possible to reverse the incorrect entry and then prepare the correct entry.** This approach will result in more entries and postings than a correcting entry, but it will accomplish the desired result.

4.4 Classified Balance Sheet

The financial statements illustrated up to this point are purposely kept simple. We classify items as assets, liabilities, and owner's equity in the balance sheet, and as revenues and expenses in the income statement. **Financial statements, however, become more useful to management, creditors, and potential investors when the elements are classified into significant subgroups.**

4.4.1 Standard Classifications

A classified balance sheet usually contains these standard classifications:

Assets	Liabilities and Owner's Equity
Current assets	Current liabilities
Long-term investments	Long-term liabilities
Property, plant, and equipment	Owner's (Stockholders' equity)
Intangible assets	

These sections help the financial statement user determine such matters as ① the availability of assets to meet debts as they come due and ② the claims of short-and long-term creditors on total assets. A classified balance sheet also makes it easier in comparing companies in the same industry, such as **GM, Ford,** and **Daimler Chrysler** in the automobile industry. Each of the sections is explained below.

(1) Current Assets

Current assets are cash and other resources that are reasonably expected to be realized in cash or sold or consumed in the business within one year of the balance sheet date or the company's operating cycle, whichever is longer. For example, accounts receivable are current assets because they will be realized in cash through collection within one year. A prepayment such as supplies is a current asset because of its expected use or consumption in the business within one year.

The operating cycle of a company is the average time that is required to go from cash to cash in producing revenues. The term "cycle" suggests a circular flow, which in this case, starts and ends with cash. For example, in municipal transit companies, the operating cycle would tend to be short since services are provided entirely on a cash basis. On the other hand, the operating cycle in manufacturing companies is longer: They purchase goods and materials, manufacture and sell products, bill customers, and collect cash. This is a cash to cash cycle that may extend for several months. Most companies have operating cycles of less than one year.

In a service enterprise, it is customary to recognize four types of current assets: ①cash, ②short-term investment such as U. S. government bonds, ③receivables (notes receivable, accounts receivable, and interest receivable), and ④prepaid expenses (insurance and supplies).

These items are listed in the order of liquidity. That is, they are listed the order in which they are expected to be converted into cash. This arrangement is illustrated below in the presentation of **UAL, Inc. (United Airlines).**

UAL, INC. (UNITED AIRLINES)
Balance Sheet (partial)
(in millions)

Current Assets	
Cash	$ 310
Short-term investments	379
Receivables	1,284
Aircraft fuel, spare parts, and supplies	340
Prepaid expenses	368
Other current assets	254
Total current assets	$ 2,935

A company's current assets are important in assessing the company's short-term debt-paying ability.

(2) Long-term Investments

Like current assets, long-term investments are resources that can be realized in cash. However, the conversion into cash is not expected within one year or the operating cycle, whichever is longer. In addition, long-term investments are not intended for use or consumption within the business. This category, often just called "investments", normally includes stocks and bonds of other corporations. **UAL, Inc. (United Airlines)** reported the following in its balance sheet.

UAL, INC. (UNITED AIRLINES)
Balance Sheet (partial)

Long-term Investments		
Investment in stock of data card corporation	$ 20,468,000	
Other long-term investment	16,961,000	$ 37,429,000

(3) Property, Plant and Equipment

Property, plant and equipment are tangible resources of a relatively permanent nature that are used in the business, such as office equipment, delivery equipment, and furniture and fixtures. Assets subject to depreciation should be reported at cost less accumulated depreciation. This practice is illustrated in the following presentation of **Delta Air Lines**.

DELTA AIR LINES, INC.
Balance Sheet (partial)
(in millions)

Property, plant, and equipment			
Flight equipment	$ 9,619		
Less: Accumulated depreciation	3,510	$ 6,109	
Ground property and equipment	3,032		
Less: Accumulated depreciation	1,758	1,274	$ 7,383

(4) Intangible Assets

Intangible assets are non-current resources that do not have physical substance. They are recorded at cost, and this cost is expensed over the useful life of the intangible asset. Intangible assets include patents, copyrights, and trademarks or trade names that give the holder **exclusive right** of use for a specified period of time. Their value to a company is generally derived from the rights or privileges granted by governmental authority.

In its balance sheet, **Brunswick Corporation** reported the following.

BRUNSWICK CORPORATION
Balance Sheet (partial)

Intangible assets	
Patents, trademarks, and other intangibles	$ 10,460,000

(5) Current Liabilities

Listed first in the liabilities and owner's equity section of the balance sheet are current liabilities. **Current liabilities** are obligations that are reasonably expected to be paid from existing current assets or through the creation of other current liabilities. As in the case of current assets, the time period for payment is one year or the operating cycle, whichever is longer. Current liabilities include ① debts related to the operating cycle, such as accounts payable and wages and salaries payable, and ② other short-term debts, such as bank loans payable, interest payable, taxes payable, and current maturities of long-term obligations (payments to be made within the next year on long-term obligations).

The arrangement of items within the current liabilities section has evolved through custom rather than from a prescribed rule. Notes payable is usually listed first, followed by accounts payable. Other items are then listed in any order. The current liabilities section adapted from the balance sheet of **UAL, Inc. (United Airlines)** is as follows.

UAL, INC. (UNITED AIRLINES)

Balance Sheet (partial)

(in thousands)

Current liabilities	
Notes payable	$ 297,518
Accounts payable	382,967
Current maturities of long-term obligations	81,525
Unearned ticket revenue	432,979
Salaries and wages payable	435,622
Taxes payable	80,390
Other current liabilities	240,652
Total current liabilities	$1,951,653

Users of financial statements look closely at the relationship between current assets and current liabilities. This relationship is important in evaluating a company's **liquidity**—its ability to pay obligations that are expected to become due within the next year or operating cycle. When current assets exceed current liabilities at the balance sheet date, the likelihood for paying the liabilities is favorable. When the reverse is true, short-term creditors may not be paid, and the company may ultimately be forced into bankruptcy.

(6) Long-term Liabilities

Obligations expected to be paid after one year or an operating cycle, whichever is longer, are classified as **long-term liabilities**. Liabilities in this category include bonds payable, mortgages payable, long-term notes payable, lease liabilities, and obligations under employee pension plans. Many companies report long-term debt maturing after one year as a single amount in the balance sheet. They then show the details of the debt in the notes that accompany the financial statements. Others list the various sources of long-term liabilities. In its balance sheet, **Consolidated FreightWAYS, Inc.** reported the following.

CONSOLIDATED FREIGHTWAYS, INC.

Balance Sheet (partial)

(in thousands)

Long-term liabilities	
Bank notes payable	$10,000
Mortgage payable	2,900
Bonds payable	53,422
Other long-term debt	9,597
Total long-term liabilities	$75,919

(7) Owner's Equity

The content of the owner's equity section varies with the form of business organization. In a proprietorship, there is one capital account. In a partnership, there is a capital account for each partner. For a corporation, owner's equity is divided into two accounts—Capital Stock and Retained Earnings. Investments of assets in the business by the stockholders are recorded by debiting an asset account and crediting the Capital Stock account. The Capital Stock and Retained Earnings accounts are combined and reported as **stockholders' equity** on the balance sheet. (We'll learn more about these corporation accounts in later **units**.)

In its balance sheet, **Dell Computer Corporation** recently reported its owner's (stockholders') equity section as follows.

DELL COMPUTER CORPORATION
(in thousands)

Stockholders' equity	
Common stock, 2,543,000,000 shares	$1,781,000
Retained earnings	540,000
Total stockholders' equity	$2,321,000

4.4.2 Classified Balance Sheet

Using the same adjusting trial balance accounts at October 31, 2012, we can prepare the classified balance sheet shown below. For illustrative purposes, assume that $1,000 of the notes payable is due currently and $4,000 is long-term.

The balance sheet is most often presented in **report form**, with assets listed above liabilities and owner's equity. The balance sheet may also be presented in **account form**: the assets section is placed on the left and liabilities and owner's equity section on the right.

FRANKLIN CORPORATION
Balance Sheet
October 31, 2012
Assets

Current assets				
Cash			$6,600	
Short-term investments			2,000	
Accounts receivable			7,000	
Inventories			4,000	
Supplies			2,100	
Prepaid insurance			400	
Total current assets			$22,100	
Long-term investments				
Investment in stock of Walters Corp			7,200	
Property, plant, and equipment				
Land			10,000	
Office equipment	$24,000			
Less: Accumulated depreciation		5,000	19,000	29,000
Intangible assets				
Patents			3,100	
Total assets			$61,400	

Liabilities and Owner's Equity

Current liabilities		
Notes payable	$11,000	
Accounts payable	2,100	
Unearned revenue	900	
Salaries payable	1,600	
Interest payable	450	
Total current liabilities	$16,050	
Long-term liabilities		
Notes payable	1,300	

Key Words and Expressions

1. accounting cycle — 会计循环
2. work sheet — 工作底稿
3. closing entries — 结账分录
4. income summary account — 收入汇总账户
5. temporary account — 临时性账户
6. permanent account — 永久性账户
7. current asset — 流动资产
8. long-term investments — 长期投资
9. intangible asset — 无形资产
10. current liabilities — 流动负债
11. long-term liabilities — 长期负债
12. government bounds — 政府债券
13. plant — 厂房
14. exclusive right — 专有权
15. physical substance — 实物形态
16. patent — 专利权
17. copyright — 版权，著作权
18. trademark — 商标权
19. liquidity — 流动性
20. stockholder's equity — 股东权益

Exercises

Case 1

The ledger of Giovanni Company includes the following unadjusted balances: Prepaid Insurance $4,000, Service Revenue $58,000, and Salaries Expense $25,000. Adjusting entries are required for (a) expired insurance $1,200; (b) services provided $900, but unbilled and uncollected; and (c) accrued salaries payable $800. Enter the unadjusted balances and adjustment into a work sheet and complete the work sheet for all accounts. Note: You will need to add the following accounts: Accounts Receivable, Salaries Payable, and Insurance Expense.

Case 2

The ledger of Benson Company contains the following balance: D. Benson, Capital $30,000; D. Benson, Drawing $2,000; Service Revenue $50,000; Salaries Expense $26,000 and Supplies Expense $4,000. Prepare the closing entries at December 31.

Case 3

The income statement for Edgebrook Golf Club for the month ending July 31 shows

Green Fee Revenue $14,000, Salaries Expense $8,200, Maintenance Expense $2,500, and Net Income $3,000. Prepare the entries to close the revenue and expense accounts. Post the entries to the revenue and expense accounts, and complete the closing process for these accounts using the three-column account.

Extended Reading

Ethics as It Applies to Accounting

The word "ethics" can mean many things to many people, but to accounting it has meaning similar to principles, morals and beliefs, as they relate to professional conduct.

The Accounting Professional and Ethical Standards Board (APESB) has issued *APES110Code of Ethics for Professional Accounting*. This code became operative on July 1st, 2006 and replaces the *Code of Ethics* of the National Institute of Accountants, the *Code of Professional Conduct* of CPA Australia and the Institute of Chartered Accountants in Australia (ICAA). The requirement that accountants conduct themselves ethically and act in a professional manner relates to behavior in the areas of the following aspects.

Integrity: the need to maintain a straightforward, honest, truthful and fair approach to professional work.

Objectivity: the need to be fair and not allow conflicts of interest, under influence of others or bias to override objectivity.

Professional competence and due care: the need to perform professional services diligently in accordance with applicable technical and professional standards as well as to maintain a high level of professional knowledge and skill.

Confidentiality: the need to respect the Confidentiality of information acquired in the course of work and not to disclose information to a third party without specific authority or unless there is a legal or professional duty to disclose it; not using confidential information for personal advantage or the advantage of third parties.

Professional behavior: the need to conduct consistent with the good reputation and to refrain from any conduct that might bring discredit to the profession.

Unit 5
Current Assets

Learning Objectives

After studying this unit, you should be able to:
1. Explain cash and the accounting treatment of cash;
2. Introduce four inventory valuation methods;
3. Explain two systems of inventory accounting;
4. Discuss the bad debt and the accounting treatment;
5. Make allowance for doubtful account receivable;
6. Write off an un-collectible account receivable.

5.1 Cash and Cash Equivalents

5.1.1 Cash

Cash is money in the form of bills or coins, which can prompt payment for goods or services in currency or by check. Cash is listed first in the balance sheet, because it is the most liquid of all current assets.

Accountants define cash as the money on deposit in banks and any items that banks will accept for immediate deposit. These items include not only coins and paper money, but also checks and money orders. On the other hand, notes receivable, IOUs, and postdated checks are not accepted for immediate deposit and are not included in the definition of cash.

In the balance sheet, cash is listed first among the current assets, because it is the most current and liquid of all assets. The banker, credit manager, or investor who studies a balance sheet critically is always interested in the total amount of cash as compared with other balance sheet items, such as accounts receivable.

5.1.2 Deposit

(1) Bank Deposit, Duplicate

The money a business receives, both cash and cheque, should be banked. It should not be used to pay for any purchases. Payments should be made separately by cheque; otherwise it will not be known how much has been received or how much has been paid by the business when reporting the profit or loss of the business.

The total of all monies received is to be banked; the total of the receipts, the total of the cash sales, and the total of the cash registers. Banking should occur on a regular basis, usually once a day. From a control basis, the bank deposit should be prepared with a duplicate and the bank should stamp the duplicate, which is then held by the business to indicate that the bank has received the money from the business for that day. This bank-stamped duplicate deposit must be sighted and signed by a senior authorised employee to confirm that there have been no alterations to the carbon copy, which can be an indication that there may have been a substitution of cheques deposited. This could indicate an attempt to falsify business records for illegal reasons.

The receipt of money by one business is due to a payment by another business.

(2) Bank Deposit Process and Duplicate Receipt

A receipt is an acknowledgment that a business has received a sum of money for a reason such as a sale of goods for cash, money owed or money earned.

Money received results in a receipt which is being prepared. The money should be banked on a daily or regular basis. The amount of the bank deposit should agree with the value of the receipts written.

If there is only one receipt written for that day, then the bank deposit will be the same as the receipt amount.

If there is more than one receipt written for that day, then the bank deposit agrees with the total of those receipts; there may be many receipts for the day but there is only one bank deposit for the day.

(3) Bank Statement and Bank Reconciliation

Since all cash receipts are to be deposited intact in the bank and all significant cash disbursements are to be made by check through the bank, each month the bank will provide the depositor with a bank statement of the depositor's account accompanied by the check, paid and charged to the account during the month. A bank statement shows the balance on deposit at the beginning of the month, the deposits and the checks paid during the month and the ending balance at the end of the month.

The balance shown on the monthly statement received from the bank will usually not agree with the balance of cash shown by the depositor's accounting records. Certain transactions recorded by the depositor will not yet have been recorded by the bank. For instance, some checks may be written by the depositor and deducted from the cash account on the depositor's records but not yet presented to the bank for payment, deposits in transit, and so on. In order to assure that the bank and the depositor are in agreement on the amount of money on deposit, a bank reconciliation (Sheet 1) needs to be prepared, because the bank and the depositor maintain independent records of deposits, the checks and the running balances of bank account. Once a month, an employee prepares a bank reconciliation to verify that these two independent sets of records are in agreement. For strong internal control, the employee who prepares the bank reconciliation should not have access to cash or be responsible for recording cash transactions in the accounting records.

Sheet 1　The Bank Reconciliation
December 31, 2014

Items	Amount	Items	Amount
Balance per bank statement		Balance per book	
Add: deposits not yet credited by bank		Add: items credited by bank not yet entered on books	
Less: outstanding check		Less: items changed by bank not yet entered on books	
Adjusted balance		Adjusted balance	

5.1.3　Petty Cash Fund

As emphasized earlier, a basic principle of internal control is that all payments should be made by cheque or electronic transfer. However, to avoid the expense and inconvenience of writing many cheques to cover minor or petty expenses for things like postage stamps and miscellaneous supplies, most entities establish a **petty cash fund**—a specified amount of cash, placed under the control of a specific employee (the petty cashier)—for making small payments.

(1) **Establishing the Fund**

The petty cash fund is established by writing a cheque to be given to the petty cashier who cashes the cheque and places the proceeds in a lockable box to which only they have access. The fund is generally established for a round amount, such as $100 or $200, expected to be sufficient to handle petty cash payments for a relatively short period such as a month. The cheque is recorded by a debit to a Petty Cash account and a credit to the Cash at Bank account. For example, assuming a fund of $100 is established on 2 January, the journal entry (in general journal format) is:

If special journals are being used, the entry to record the establishment of the petty cash fund is made in the cash payments journal. Petty Cash is entered in the account column and the amount of $100 is entered in the cash at bank and other accounts columns. After posting, the effect is the same as for the general journal entry, ie the Petty Cash account in the general ledger is debited and the Cash at Bank account is credited.

(2) **Making Payments from the Fund**

As cash payments are made from the fund, the recipient signs a **petty cash voucher** or **receipt** prepared by the petty cashier. The voucher shows the amount paid, the purpose of the payment and the date of the payment. A voucher is prepared for every payment made from the fund and is placed in the petty cash box. Outlays on most of the expenses and minor assets covered by petty cash payments will include GST. The petty cashier must ensure that expenses are recorded at GST—exclusive amounts, and that adequate records are made of any GST outlays associated with these expenses. Thus, at all times the total of the vouchers plus cash in the fund should be equal to the amount originally placed in the fund, $100 in our illustration. The following figure shows an example of a petty cash voucher.

PETTY CASH VOUCHER

No. **2** DATE **15 January 2013** AMOUNT **$13.53**

PURPOSE *Miscellaneous office supplies*

GST included $1.23

DEBIT TO *Office Expenses*

APPROVED BY ✍ *J.B. Small*

Petty cashier

(3) Reimbursing the Fund

Because payments from the fund will gradually decrease the cash available, the petty cashier must be reimbursed periodically by writing a cheque equal to the amount of the sum of the vouchers in the fund. Each voucher stamped *paid* by the cashier (or printed as *being paid* when processed by the computer system). The cheque is cashed by the cashier of the fund and the proceeds are placed in the petty cash box. Various expense accounts are debited as indicated by the petty cash vouchers, the GST Outlays account is debited for the GST, and the Cash at Bank is credited for the amount needed to reimburse the fund. For example, the petty cash box had vouchers and cash at the end of the first month of operations as shown below:

Voucher No.	Purpose	GST	Amount	Total
1	Postage stamps	$ 3.00	$ 30.00	$ 33.00
2	Office supplies	1.23	12.30	13.53
3	Postage	2.65	26.47	29.12
4	Stationery	1.52	15.22	16.74
	Cash in box			7.61
		$ 8.40	$ 83.99	$ 100.00

Because the cash in the fund is low, the petty cashier is reimbursed and the following entry (in general journal format) is made:

Jan. 31	Stationery Expense	15.22	
	Office Supplies Expense	12.30	
	Postage Expense	56.47	
	GST Outlays	8.40	
	Cash at Bank		92.39

Since the petty cash vouchers are supplementary records, this entry is needed so that the expenses are properly recorded and posted to general ledger accounts. Thus, expense accounts and the GST Outlays account are debited when the fund is replenished. Note that the

Petty Cash account is not affected by the reimbursement entry. The Petty Cash account is debited only when the fund is initially established, and no other entries are made to the Petty Cash account unless a decision is made to increase or decrease the size of the fund. The petty cash fund is normally included with other cash amounts and reported as a single amount on the balance sheet.

The petty cash fund is also reimbursed at the end of an accounting period, even if the amount of cash in the fund is not running low, in order to have the expenses represented by the vouchers in the fund plus the GST outlayed recorded during the current accounting period. If the fund is not reimbursed, cash will be overstated in the balance sheet and expenses will be understated in the income statement for the period.

On occasion, the petty cashier may forget to obtain a signed voucher for a payment from the fund, in which case the fund will be short. When this occurs, the Cash Short and Over account is debited for the shortage when the fund is replenished.

If special journals are being used, the above entry for reimbursement of the petty cash fund is entered in the cash payments journal. Reimbursement is done by drawing a cheque for the total amount of the petty cash vouchers used (ie cash spent) during the period, and this cheque has to be recorded in the cash payments journal along with all other cheques written. When the reimbursement is recorded in a payments journal, the entry is shown as below (selected columns only):

DATE	Account Debited	Chq No.	Post Ref	Debits		Credits	
				GST Outlays	Other	Cash at Bank	Discount Received
Jan 31	Stationery		530	1.52	15.22		
	Office Supplies Exp		515	1.23	12.30		
	Postage Exp	140	572	5.65	56.50	92.39	

Note that the effect on the general ledger accounts is exactly the same as that for the general journal—the appropriate expense accounts are debited, GST Outlays is debited for the total of $8.40, and the Cash at Bank account is credited.

5.2 Accounts Receivable

Accounts receivable are very liquid assets, usually being converted into cash within a period of 30 to 60 days. So, accounts receivable from customers (and notes receivable as well) classified as current assets appear in the balance sheet immediately after cash and cash equivalents.

Accounts receivable arise when a business sells goods and services on credit. Sales and profits can be increased by granting customers the privilege of making payment a month or more after the date of sale. However, no business concerned wants to sell on credit to the customer who will prove unable or unwilling to pay his or her account. Consequently, most business organizations have a credit department which investigates the credit worthiness of each prospective customer.

5.2.1 Significance of Accounts Receivable

Regardless of how thoroughly the credit department investigates prospective customers, some uncollectible accounts will arise as a result of errors in judgment or because of unexpected development. In fact, a limited amount of uncollectible accounts is evidence of a sound credit policy. If the credit department should become too cautious and conservative in rating customers, it might avoid all credit losses, but, in so doing, lose profitable business by rejecting many acceptable customers.

5.2.2 Allowance for Doubtful Accounts

There is no way of telling in advance which accounts receivable will be collected and which one will prove to be worthless. It is therefore impossible to credit the account of any particular customer to reflect the overall estimate of the year's credit losses. Neither is it possible to credit the accounts receivable controlling account in the general ledger. If the accounts receivable controlling account were to be credited with the estimated amount of doubtful accounts, this controlling account would no longer be in balance with the total of the numerous customer accounts in the subsidiary ledger. The only practicable alternative, therefore, is to credit a separate account called **Allowance for Doubtful Accounts** with the amount estimated to be uncollectible.

The Allowance for Doubtful Accounts is often described as a contra-asset account or a valuation account. Both of these terms indicate that the Allowance for Doubtful Accounts has a credit balance, which is offset against the **Accounts Receivable** account to produce the proper balance sheet value for this asset.

【Example for the Allowance Method of Accounting for Bad Debts】

We will look at an example to see how the allowance method is done in practice. A company that specializes in training services incurred the following transactions that pertain to 2014:

① Recognized $6,000 of service revenue earned on account;

② Collected $3,600 cash from accounts receivable;

③ Recognized $400 of bad debt expense for accounts receivable that are expected to be uncollectible in the future.

Key:

① The first transaction is already familiar to us. Assets (Account Receivable) and equities (Service Revenue) increase by the like amount;

② The collection of accounts receivable acts to decrease one asset (Accounts Receivable) and increase another (Cash);

③ Usually a company cannot know for sure how much of accounts receivable will be doubtful in the future. In such a cash, nevertheless, it is reasonable to make an estimate. For example, in our illustration the owner of the company is not able to say exactly how much of $2,400 (ie, $6,000 — $3,600 already collected) of the accounts receivable will be collected or how much will be not. But the owner can estimate that, let us say, clients will not pay $400 of receivables in the current accounting period. For this purpose an adjusting entry is required:

The amount of accounts receivable that is expected to be uncollectible ($400) is recorded in a special contra asset account called **Allowance for Doubtful Debts**. The balance of this account is subtracted from Accounts Receivable to receivable value of receivables (which is added to the total assets in the balance sheet):

Accounts Receivable	$2,400
Less: Allowance for Doubtful Debts	(400)
Net Receivable Value of Receivables	$2,000

Recall that the net realizable value is the amount of receivable a company actually expects to get in the future.

The General Journal and T-accounts

The transactions and the closing entry are shown in the general journal as follows:

Date	Account Titles	Debit	Credit
1	Accounts Receivable	60,000	
	Service Revenue		60,000
	To record service revenue earned on account		
2	Cash	3,600	
	Accounts Receivable		3,600
	To record Collected cash from accounts receivable		
3	Bad Debts Expense	400	
	Allowance Receivable		400
	To record recognized bad debt expense		
4	Service Revenue	6,000	
	Bad Debts Expense		400
	Retained Earning		5,600
	To transfer Revenue and Expense to Retained Earning account		

5.2.3 How Is the Amount of Allowance for Doubtful Debts Estimated?

In the illustration above we assumed the amount of allowance for doubtful debts ($400). However, how is it estimated in reality? Usually, accountants use records from previous years and adjust it to current situations. For example, in preceding accounting periods of a business receivables that appeared to doubtful amounted to 5% of the total accounts receivable. However, in this accounting period it is expected that a bigger amount will not be collected since there were many purchases by customers with bad credit history. In this collection, the accountants decide to increase this percentage to 7. So, if the company has the ending balance of the accounts receivable of $2,400 then the allowance for doubtful debts will be $168 (ie, $2,400×7%), and the net realizable value will be $18,600 ($20,000−$1,400). The last sum is included in total assets.

There are three methods of estimating uncollectible accounts (sometimes called bad debt) expense: one is referred to as the balance sheet approach and rests on **an aging of the accounts receivable**, the second approach is regarded as the income statement approach and computes the uncollectible accounts as **a percentage of the year's net sales**, and the last approach is called *the direct write-off method*.

(1) Aging the Accounts Receivable

A past-due account receivable is always viewed with some suspicion. The fact that a receivable is past due suggests that the customer is either unable or unwilling to pay. The analysis of accounts receivable by age is known as aging the accounts, as illustrated by the schedule below (Sheet 2).

Sheet 2　Analysis of Accounts Receivable by Age
December 31, 2014

Customers	Total	Not yet due	1~30 days past due	31~60 days past due	61~90 days past due	Over 90 days past due
Customers—A	1,000	1,000				
Customers—B	300			300		
Customers—C	1,600	1,600				
Customers—D	1,800				1,600	200
Customers—E	800	800				
others	64,500	32,600	20,000	8,400	400	3,100
Totals	70,000	36,000	20,000	8,700	2,000	3,300
percentage/%	100	51	29	12	3	5

The longer past due an account receivable becomes, the greater the likelihood that it will not be collected in full. In recognition of this fact, the analysis of receivables by age groups can be used as a stepping stone in determining a reasonable amount to add to the probable expense for each age group of accounts receivable (Sheet 3). This percentage, when applied to the dollar amount in each age group, gives a probable expense for each group. By adding together the probable expense for all the age groups, the required balance in the Allowance totals from the preceding illustration and shows how the total probable expense from uncollectible accounts is computed.

Sheet 3　Accounts Receivable by Age Groups

Period	Amount	Percentage considered uncollectible	Probable uncollectible accounts
Not yet due	$36,000	1	$360
1～30 days past due	20,000	3	600
31～60 days past due	8,700	10	870
61～90 days past due	2,000	20	400
Over 90 days past due	3,300	50	1,625
Total	$70,000	—	$3,880

【Transaction 5-1】

Assume that an Allowance for Doubtful Accounts of $3,880 is required. The accounting entry is as below:

Dec. 31	Uncollectible Accounts Expenses	3,880	
	Allowance for Accounts		3,880
	(To record uncollectible accounts expenses $3,880)		

(2) Estimating Uncollectible Accounts as a Percentage of Net Sales

An alternative approach preferred by some companies consists of computing the charge to uncollectible accounts expenses as a percentage of the net sales for the year. The question to be answered is not "How large a valuation allowance is needed to reduce our receivables to realizable value?" Instead, the question is stated as "How much uncollectible accounts expense is associated with this year's volume of sales?"

【Transaction 5-2】

Assume that for several years the expenses of uncollectible accounts has averaged 1% of net sales (sales minus sales returns and allowances and sales discounts). At the end of the current year, the following account balances appear in the ledger.

	Dr.	Cr.
Sales		$2,520,000
Sales Returns and Allowances	$80,000	
Sales Discounts	$40,000	
Net Sales		$2,400,000

The net sales of the current year amount to $2400,000; 1% of this amount is $24,000. The accounting entry is as below:

Dec. 31	Uncollectible Accounts Expenses	24,000	
	Allowance for Doubtful Accounts		24,000
	(To record uncollectible accounts expenses as a percentage of the net sales for the year $24,000)		

If a company makes both cash sales and credit sales, it is better to exclude the cash sales from consideration and to compute the percentage relationship of uncollectible accounts expenses to credit sales only.

This approach of estimating uncollectible accounts receivable as a percentage of credit sales is easier to apply than the method of aging accounts receivable. The aging of receivables, however, tends to give a more reliable estimate of uncollectible accounts because of the consideration given to the age and collectible of the specific accounts receivable at the balance sheet date. Some companies use the income statement approach for preparing monthly financial statements and internal reports, but use the balance sheet method for preparing annual financial statements.

These two methods belong to the allowance method. An alternative to the allowance method is the direct write-off method.

(3) Direct Write-off Method

Some companies do not use any valuation allowance for accounts receivable. Instead of making end-of-period adjusting entries to record uncollectible accounts expenses on the basis of estimates, these companies recognize no uncollectible accounts expenses until specific receivables are determined to be worthless. This method makes no attempt to match revenue and related expenses. Uncollectible accounts expenses are recorded in the period in which individual accounts receivable are determined to be worthless rather than in the period in which the sales were made.

When a particular customer's account is determined to be uncollectible written off directly to Uncollectible Accounts Expense, it can be recorded as follows:

Dec. 31	Uncollectible Accounts Expense	500	
	Accounts Receivable		500
	(To record having written off the accounts receivable's bad debt expense of $ 250)		

When the direct write-off method is in use, the accounts receivable will be listed in the balance sheet at their gross amount, and no valuation allowance will be used. The receivables, therefore, are not stated at estimated net realizable value.

In some situations, use of the direct write-off method is acceptable. If a company makes most of its sales for cash, the amount of its accounts receivable will be small in relation to other assets. The expense from uncollectible accounts should also be small.

Consequently, the direct write-off method is acceptable because its use does not have a material effect on the reported net income. Another situation in which the direct write-off method works satisfactorily is in a company which sells all or most of its output to a few large companies which are financially strong. In this setting there may be no basis for making advance estimates of any credit losses.

5.3 Inventory

Inventory refers to various assets that are stocked for the purpose of sale, production or consumption during the process of the production and operation for a business. The definition of inventory is applied to manufacturing enterprises as well as merchandising enterprises. For a merchandising enterprise, inventory consists of all goods owned and held for sale in the regular course of business. In manufacturing enterprises, there are three major types of inventories: raw materials, goods in process, and finished goods. Since inventories will typically be sold within a year or during a firm's normal operating cycle if it should be longer than a year, inventories are classified as current assets. In the balance sheet, inventory is listed immediately after receivables.

5.3.1 Two Kinds of Inventory Systems

The two major alternative accounting systems for determining the value of inventory and the cost of goods sold are called perpetual inventory system and periodic inventory system.

(1) Perpetual Inventory System

In a perpetual inventory system, each receipt and each issue of an inventory item is recorded in the inventory records to maintain an up-to-date perpetual inventory balance at all times. The result of the perpetual system is verified at least once a year by physically counting the inventory and matching the count to the accounting records. Thus, the perpetual inventory records provide the units and costs of inventory and cost of goods sold at any time. The unit costs applied to each issue or sale is determined by the cost flow assumption used.

The advantage of a perpetual inventory system is that, theoretically, it is possible to determine the value of inventory on hand and the cost of goods sold for the period without performing an inventory count. The use of a perpetual inventory system allows management to balance the inventory on hand with manufacturing business needs and customers' requirements.

(2) Periodic Inventory System

A business entity using a periodic inventory system does not maintain a detailed record of each inventory transaction. The purchases of inventory are recorded in the accounting records, just as they are under the perpetual inventory system. However, when sales of inventory are made, only the Sales revenue entry is made. There is no entry made to reduce the inventory account and to record cost of goods sold. That means that the Inventory account is not up to date during the period since it only records the beginning balance and purchase of inventory, but not the consumption of inventory. At the end of the period, a physical count of inventories is taken to arrive at the ending inventory in units and dollars.

A periodic system tends to be easier to maintain and is less expensive than a perpetual system. However, one of the disadvantages of a periodic system is that its inability to distinguish between goods that have been sold and goods that have been stolen. The ending inventory is derived using the physical count; the underlying assumption is that if it is not there, it has been sold. On the other hand, a perpetual system "knows" what should be there; if it is not, then it is deemed to have been stolen.

(3) Comparison of the Accounting Recording Procedures under the Two Kinds of Inventory Systems

The accounting recording procedures are different under the periodic inventory system and the perpetual inventory system. The periodic system of inventory accounting requires that acquisition of merchandise be recorded by debits to a purchases account. At the date of a sales transaction, no entry is made to record the cost of the merchandise that has been sold. Consequently, a physical inventory must be taken in order to determine the cost of the ending inventory at the end of an accounting. Under the perpetual inventory system, as merchandise is purchased, its cost is debited to an inventory account; as merchandise is sold, its cost is transferred out of inventory account and into a cost of goods sold account.

Note that the inventory account under a perpetual system is increased by purchases and decreased by the cost of goods sold, purchases returns and allowances, and discounts. Therefore, at the end of the period the only adjustment made is to bring the inventory account balance into agreement with the amount of the physical inventory. While under a periodic system, the inventory account does not change at the usual time. The amount of the ending inventory is produced after the adjusting entries are only made at the end of the period.

The following entries demonstrate the recording procedures to be followed under the perpetual inventory system, as contrasted with the periodic system (Sheet 4).

Sheet 4 The Different Accounting Practices under Two Kinds of Inventory Systems

Periodic inventory system	Perpetual inventory system
(1) Purchased $5,000 worth of merchandise on account; term 2/10. n/30	
Purchase 5,000 　　Accounts Payable 5,000	Inventory 5,000 　　Accounts Payable 5,000
(2) Returned $1,000 merchandise to vendors	
Accounts Payable 1,000 　　Purchases Returns and Allowances 1,000	Accounts Payable 1,000 　　Inventory 1,000
(3) Paid for merchandise (discount taken)	
Accounts Payable 4,000 　　Purchases Discount 800 　　Cash 3,200	Accounts Payable 4,000 　　Inventory 800 　　Cash 3,200
(4) Sold goods, costing $1,200 for $2,000	
Accounts Receivable 2,000 　　Sales 2,000	Accounts Receivable 2,000 　　Sales 2,000 Cost of Goods Sold 1,200 　　Inventory 1,200

(5) Counted inventory at the end of period is $50,000. The balance in the inventory account under the periodic inventory system is $20,000 (the beginning inventory). The balance in the inventory account under the perpetual inventory system is $50,800.

| Continued

Periodic inventory system	Perpetual inventory system

Income Summary   20,000
    Inventory   20,000
Inventory   5,000
    Income Summary   5,000
	Loss on Inventory Shortage 800
	    inventory 800

5.3.2 Methods of Determining Inventory Costs

In practice a situation when inventory is purchased at different prices occurs often, which explains the question of which cost to allocate cost of goods sold versus ending inventory appears. There are four common inventory cost flow methods that provide solutions to the problem and answer the question. The four methods are:

① Specific identification;
② Weighted-average;
③ First-in, first-out (FIFO);
④ Last-in, first-out (LIFO).

(1) Specific Identification Method

The specific identification method (also known as specific invoice) requires the recording of detailed information for each purchase transaction so that merchandise on hand at the end of an accounting period can be identified with a specific order. Each purchase may be assigned a special number, or a special tag may be placed on each specific order so that each sale can be identified to the related invoice. In this way, the merchandise on hand may be obtained from the purchase invoice.

The specific identification method is best suited to inventories of high-value, low-volume items. New automobiles and construction equipment are good examples. The method of pricing inventory is required to identify the units in the ending inventory as coming from specific purchases. Specific identification is not feasible where products are of a small unit price and involve large volumes. If the units in the ending inventory can be identified as coming from specific purchases, they may be priced at the amounts listed on the purchase invoices.

【Transaction 5-3】

Assume that ABC company had such ending balances in its accounts:

Assets			Claims		
Cash	+	Inventory	Contributed Capital	+	Retained Earnings
$9,000	+	0	$9,000	+	0

ABC Company uses the specific invoice method for valuing the ending inventory. During its first year in business, the following purchases of merchandise were made:

Purchase date	Quantity	Unit price	Total cost
Jan. 20	100 sets	$6.00	$600
Apr. 11	400 sets	6.50	2,600
Jul. 20	400 sets	6.25	2,500
Sept. 15	100 sets	6.60	660
Total	1,000 sets		$6,360

During the year, 880 sets of merchandise were sold for $8,800 and 120 sets were on hand at the end of the year. The 120 bags in the ending inventory could be specifically identified as 60 sets acquired on September 15 and 60 sets acquired on July 20.

Cost of ending inventory $= 60 \times 6.6 + 60 \times 6.25 = \$771$

Cost of goods sold $= 100 \times 6 + 400 \times 6.5 + 340 \times 6.25 + 40 \times 6.6 = \$5,589$

(2) **Weighted-average Method**

Weighted-average method of valuing inventory recognizes that prices will vary as merchandise is purchased during the fiscal period. Therefore, under this method the units in the ending inventory are priced at the average unit cost of the merchandise on hand during the entire fiscal period. Before computing the value of the ending inventory using the weighted-average method, the average cost for one unit must be obtained and then applied to the number of units in the ending inventory.

【Transaction 5-4】

Using the data given in Transaction 5-3, the ending inventory under the weighted-average method is computed as follows:

Average unit cost $= \dfrac{\$6,360 \text{ total cost}}{1,000 \text{ sets purchased}} = 6.36$

Cost of ending inventory $= \$6.36 \times 120 = \$763.2$

Cost of goods sold $= \$6.36 \times 880 = 5,596.80$

(3) **First-in, First-out (FIFO) Method**

The first-in, first-out (FIFO) method of inventory valuation assumes that the first goods purchased are the first goods sold. Therefore, the merchandise on hand at the end of period would consist of the last or most recent purchase valued at the current or last purchase price.

【Transaction 5-5】

Using the data given in Transaction 5-3, the ending inventory under the FIFO method would be computed as follows:

Purchase date	Quantity	Unit price	Total cost	Remarks
Jan. 20	100 sets	$6.00	$600	Sold 100
Apr. 11	400 sets	6.50	2600	Sold 400
Jul. 20	400 sets	6.25	2500	Sold 380
				On hand 20
Sept. 15	100 sets	6.60	660	On hand 100
Total	1,000 sets		$6,360	

Cost of ending inventory by FIFO method $=100\times 6.60+20\times 6.25=\$785$

Cost of goods sold $=100\times 6.00+400\times 6.5+380\times 6.25=\$5,575$

(4) Last-in, First-out (LIFO) Method

The last-in, first-out (LIFO) method of inventory valuation assumes that the last goods purchased are the first ones sold. The goods that remain unsold at the end of the period would consist of goods in the beginning inventory and/or the first goods purchased. When using the LIFO inventory pricing method, the first items purchased are assumed to be the last items sold. Therefore, the ending inventory would be valued at the earliest or first purchase price.

【Transaction 5-6】

Using the data given in Transaction 5-3, the ending inventory under the LIFO method would be computed as follows:

Purchase date	Quantity	Unit price	Total cost	Remarks
Jan. 20	100 sets	$6.00	$600	On hand 100
Apr. 11	400 sets	6.50	2,600	On hand 20
				Sold 380
Jul. 20	400 sets	6.25	2,500	Sold 400
Sept. 15	100 sets	6.60	660	Sold 100
Total	500 bags		$6,360	

Cost of ending inventory by LIFO method $=100\times 6.00+20\times 6.50=\$730.00$

Cost of goods sold $=100\times 6.6+400\times 6.25+380\times 6.5=\$5,630$

When prices are rising, LIFO results in lower reported income and thus may provide a related tax benefit. LIFO better matches current costs against current revenues because the most recent purchases are reflected as cost of goods sold. However, it consequently processes the ending inventory at the older, less realistic unit price. Because of this, the LIFO inventory figure on the balance sheet often becomes quite meaningless in terms of current cost prices. This method is not allowed to use in IAS and Chinese GAAP any more.

5.3.3 The Differences in the Financial Statements under the Three Methods

Since the cost of inventory is allocated between the cost of goods sold and the ending inventory, the type of the cost flow method employed by a company has effects on the balance sheet as well as the income statement. FIFO transfers the first costs to the income statement while leaving the last in the balance sheet. Contrary, LIFO moves the first cost to the income statement and remains the last cost in the balance sheet. The weighted-average uses the same average costs for both income statement and balance.

Income Statement

Items	FIFO	LIFO	Weighted-average
Sales	$8,800	$8,800	$8,800
Cost of Goods Sold	(5,575)	(5,630)	(5,596.80)
Gross Margin	3,225	3,170	3,203.20
Operating Expenses	0	0	0
Income before Taxes	3,225	3,170	3,203.20
Income Tax Expense(25%)	(806.25)	(792.50)	(800.80)
Net Income	$2,418.75	$2,377.50	$2,402.40

Balance Sheet

Items	FIFO	LIFO	Weighted-average
Assets			
Cash	$10,633.75	$10,647.50	$10,639.20
Inventory	785	730	763.2
Total Assets	$11,418.75	$11,377.50	$11,402.40
Liabilities	$0	$0	$0
Equity			
Contributed Capital	$9,000	$9,000	$9,000
Retained Earnings	$2,418.75	$2,377.50	$2,402.40
Total Equity	$11,418.75	$11,377.50	$11,402.40

Statement of Cash Flows

Items	FIFO	LIFO	Weighted-average
Operating Activities			
Cash Inflow from Sales	$8,800	$8,800	$8,800
Cash Outflow for Inventory	($6,360)	($6,360)	($6,360)
Cash Outflow for Tax	(806.25)	(792.50)	(800.80)
Net Cash Flow from Operating Activities	$1,633.75	$1,647.5	$1,639.20
Investing Activities	$0	$0	$0
Financing Activities	$0	$0	$0
Net Increase in Cash	$1,633.75	$1,647.5	$1,639.20
Beginning Cash Balance	$9,000	$9,000	$9,000
Ending Cash Balance	$10,633.75	$10,647.50	$10,639.20

5.3.4 The Use of the Lower of Cost or Market Rule

Now let us get back to where we started, namely the lower of cost or market rule. So far we have been dealing with the methods applied to determine the cost flows of goods (more specifically, the cost of goods sold and the ending inventory). Once the cost of ending inventory is computed, it is required to compare it with the current market value, which is the amount that would have been paid to replace the merchandise. If the market value of ending inventory is lower than the book value of such inventory, the resultant loss must be recognized in the current period.

The lower of cost or market rule can be applied to:

(1) each individual inventory item;

(2) major classes or categories of inventory;

(3) entire cost of inventory in aggregate.

Look at the table below:

Item	Cost	Market Value	Lower of Cost or Market
A	$2,000	$2,080	$2,000
B	$1,300	$1,180	$1,180
C	$200	$100	$100
D	$34	$36	$34
In Aggregate	$3,534	$3,396	$3,314

For item A cost is lower than the market value, so the lower of cost of market is $2,000. For B, the market value is lower, so the lower of cost of market is $1,180. For items C and D, the way of determining is identical. As for aggregate, the total cost of the four items is $3,534, and their market value is $3,396. So, applying the lower of cost or market rule we need to select the market value for ending inventory ($3,314).

5.3.5 Inventory Loss

If the market value of an item (or items in aggregate) is lower than its cost, the company has to reduces its ending inventory by the amount of difference. For example, in illustration above the difference between the cost in aggregate and the market value is $138 (ie, $3,534 − $3,396). If a perpetual inventory system is used, the entry that records this reduction acts to decrease assets (Inventory) and equity (by increasing Cost of Goods Sold or Inventory Loss):

Account Titles	Debit	Credit
Cost of Goods Sold(or Inventory Loss)	138	
Inventory		138

The loss should be shown as an operating expense on the income statement. However, if the amount is immaterial, then the loss can be included in the cost of goods sold.

Under periodic inventory system, the amount of ending inventory is shown at the lower of cost or market. Any decrease in ending inventory automatically increases the cost of goods sold since the latter is computed as the difference between the cost of goods available for sale and the ending inventory. Assume the following situation when the loss is $100:

	Before applying the rule	After applying the rule
Beginning Inventory	2,000	2,000
Plus: purchases	4,600	4,600
Cost of Goods Available for Sale	6,600	6,600
Less: Ending Inventory	(1,000)	(900)
Cost of Goods Sold	5,600	5,700

Key Words and Expressions ▶▶

1. deposit 存款
2. IOU (I owe you 的缩写) 欠条，借据
3. postdated check 远期支票
4. check account 支票账户
5. ending inventory 期末存货
6. petty cash 备用金
7. bank statement 银行对账单
8. outstanding check 未兑现的支票
9. uncollectible accounts 无法收回的账款，坏账
10. allowance for doubtful accounts 坏账准备
11. bad debt 坏账，呆账

12.	balance sheet approach	资产负债表法
13.	income statement approach	利润表法
14.	aging of accounts receivable method	账龄分析法
15.	past-due accounts receivable	逾期应收账款
16.	returns and allowances	退货及折让
17.	discount	折扣
18.	allowance method	备抵法
19.	direct write-off method	直接冲销法
20.	specific identification	个别计价法
21.	first-in, first-out (FIFO)	先进先出法
22.	last-in, first-out (LIFO)	后进先出法
23.	weighted-average	加权平均法
24.	raw material	原材料
25.	goods in process	在产品
26.	finished goods	产成品
27.	perpetual inventory system	永续盘存制
28.	periodical inventory system	实地盘存制

Exercises

Case 1

The following is a record of ABC Company's transactions of Boston Teapots for the month of May 2014.

June 1: Balanced 400 units at $20.

June 15: Sold 300 units at $42.

June 23: Purchased 600 units at $25.

June 25: Sold 540 units at $42.

June 28: Purchased 400 units at $30.

Required

(1) Assume that perpetual inventories are not maintained and that a physical count at the end of the month shows 560 units on hand; calculate the cost of the ending inventory using FIFO.

(2) Assume that perpetual records are maintained and they tie into the general ledger; calculate the ending inventory using FIFO.

Case 2

ZLT Company began operations on January 1, 2012. During the next two years, the company completed a number of transactions involving credit sales, accounts receivable collections and bad debts. These transactions are summarized as follows:

Year 2012

(1) Sold merchandise on credit for $27,250, terms n/60.

(2) Wrote off uncollectible accounts receivable in the amount of $425.

(3) Received cash of $22,550 in payment of outstanding accounts receivable.

(4) In adjusting the accounts on December 31, concluded that 2% of the outstanding accounts receivable would become uncollectible.

Year 2013

(1) Sold merchandise on credit for $33,900, terms n/60.

(2) Wrote off uncollectible accounts receivable in the amount of $640.

(3) Received cash of $32,950 in payment of outstanding accounts receivable.

(4) In adjusting the accounts on December 31, concluded that 2% of the outstanding accounts receivable would become uncollectible.

Required

Prepare general journal entries to record the 2012 and 2013 summarized transactions of ZLT Company and the adjusting entries to record bad debts expenses at the end of each year.

Case 3

Assume that a company named Vivian Electric Motor had such ending balances in its accounts:

Assets			Claims		
Cash	+	Inventory	Contributed Capital	+	Retained Earnings
$10,000	+	$5,000	$10,000	+	$5,000

Now consider the following transactions that happened in year 2012:

(1) Two purchases of electric motor were made;

(2) One sale of the goods took place.

Beginning Inventory	200 units * $25	=	$5,000 (at cost)
Purchase One	200 units * $30	=	$9,000 (at cost)
Purchase Two	200 units * $40	=	$8,000 (at cost)
Sale	200 units * $100	=	$50,000 (at selling price)

In addition, at the end of the accounting period of 2012 the company paid cash for income tax at a rate of 40% of income. Remember that now we are using the perpetual inventory system.

Required

Fill these tables referencing the relevance text above.

(1) FIFO method:

Beginning Inventory		=	
Purchase One		=	
Purchase Two		=	
Total			

(2) LIFO method:

Purchase Two		=	
Purchase One		=	
Beginning Inventory		=	
Total			

(3) The differences in the financial statements under the two methods:

Item	FIFO	LIFO
Sales		
Cost of Goods Sold		
Gross Margin		
Operating Expenses		
Income before Taxes		
Income Tax Expense		
Net Income		
Assets		
Cash		
Inventory		
Total Assets		
Liabilities		
Equity		
Contributed Capital		
Retained Earnings		
Total Equity		
Operating Activities		
Cash Inflow from Sales		
Cash Outflow for Inventory		
Cash Outflow for Tax		
Net Cash Flow from Operating Activities		
Investing Activities		
Financing Activities		
Net Increase in Cash		
Beginning Cash Balance		
Ending Cash Balance		

Extended Reading

Internal Control for Accounts Receivable

Proper segregation of duties is the significance to the management of accounts receivable. In a small business, it is not uncommon to find that one employee has responsibility for handling cash receipts from customers, maintaining the accounts receivable records, issuing credit memos for goods returned by customers, and writing off receivables budged to be uncollectible. Such a combination of duties is a virtual invitation to fraud. The employee in this situation is able to remove the cash collected from a customer without making any record of the collection. The next step is to dispose of the balance in the customer's account. This can be done by issuing a credit memo indicating that the customer had returned merchandise or by writing off the customer's account as uncollectible.

To avoid fraud in handling of receivables, some of the most important rules are that employees who maintain the accounts receivable subsidiary ledger must not have access to cash receipts, and employees who handle cash receipts must not have access to the records of receivable. Furthermore, employees who maintain records of receivables must not have authority to issue credit memos or to write off receivables as uncollectible. These are classic examples of incompatible duties. In addition, documents such as sales invoices and credit memos must be serially numbered and every number in the series must be accounted for.

Unit 6
Long-Term Assets

Learning Objectives

After studying this unit, you should be able to:
1. Explain the nature and classification of plant and equipment;
2. Understand the cost of plant and equipment;
3. Describe the depreciation of plant and equipment;
4. Calculate the amount of depreciation by using different methods;
5. Explain accounting for acquisition of intangible assets;
6. Describe the amortization for intangible assets.

Long-term assets are defined as the recourses a business possesses and uses to bring forth or yield revenue and can be divided into two categories: tangible assets such as plant assets and intangible assets. Examples of such assets can be trucks for transportation companies or computers with tables and seats for software companies. What does long-term mean? As a rule, long-term refers to more than a year. So, long-term assets are those whose economic life (the period of their being used by a company) is longer than a year.

6.1 Plant and Equipment (Fixed Assets)

The term plant and equipment is used to describe long-term assets acquired for use in the operation of the business and not intended for resale to customers. Among the more common examples are land, buildings, machinery, furniture and fixtures, office equipment, and automobiles.

6.1.1 The Term of Plant and Equipment

The term fixed assets or plant assets has been used in accounting literature to describe all types of plant and equipment. This term, however, has virtually disappeared from the published financial statements of large corporations. Plant and equipment appear to be a more descriptive term. Another alternative term used on many corporation balance sheets is property, plant, and equipment. It is convenient to think of a plant and equipment as a stream of services to be received by the owner over a period of years.

6.1.2 The Cost of Plant and Equipment

All assets are recorded at their historical cost. Historical cost usually includes the purchase price, plus whatever additional costs necessary to get the asset and to prepare it for intended use. Additional costs (costs besides the purchase price) may be transportation costs, insurance while delivering the assets, etc. The following are the costs usually included in the historical costs of assets:

 Purchase of a building: purchase price, title search and transfer documents, real estate fees, remodeling costs, etc..

 Purchase of equipment: purchase price, delivery costs, installation, cost for modifications needed for intended use, etc..

 Purchase of land: purchase price, removal of old buildings, title search and transfer documents, real estate fees, etc..

However, there are a lot of expenses that cannot be added to the cost of an asset. Such expenditures include payments for fines, damages, and so on, which are not considered normal costs of obtaining an asset.

(1) **Assets Purchased for Cash**

Cost is most easily determined when an asset is purchased for cash. The cost of the asset is then equal to the cash outlay necessary in acquiring the asset plus any expenditure for freight, insurance while in transit, installation, and any other cost necessary to make the asset ready for use.

【Transaction 6-1】

A business purchased equipment on Jan. 15 for $10,000, and freight charges of $1,500, installation and other "start-up" costs amounting to $800. The business paid cash of $10,000, others would be paid within 10 days.

Jan. 15	Equipment	12,300	
	Cash		10,000
	Accounts Payable		2,300
	To record having bought new equipment,		
	some paid for cash and the balance was not paid.		

(2) **Assets Acquired by Exchange**

Assets are frequently acquired by trading in an existing asset as partial or complete payment for a new asset. The cost amount of the new asset is the money amount of the resources given up to acquire it. The resources "given up" in this case include a non-monetary asset. Determination of the cost of the new asset depends upon the measurement of the money amount of the asset traded in.

The AICPA in Opinion NO. 29 recommended that "Accounting for non-monetary transactions should be based upon the fair values."

This recommendation is based upon an assumption that where a non-monetary asset is exchanged for another, two separate transactions occur. The traded asset is realized for cash at its fair market price and the proceeds are used to acquire the new asset. The opinion thus interprets the money amount of the traded asset as the price for which it could be sold in a normal arm's-length transaction. This amount is referred to as the asset's fair market value.

【Transaction 6-2】

On Dec. 20, ABC corporation exchanged old equipment with a cost of $100,000, accumulated depreciation of $70,000, and a fair market value of $25,000 and $95,000 for new equipment with a fair market value of $120,000 without considering added-value tax.

Dec. 20	Equipment	120,000	
	Accumulated Depreciation	70,000	
	Loss on Disposal of Equipment	5,000	
	Cash		95,000
	Equipment		100,000
	To record the business of exchanging old equipment for new one.		

(3) **Donated Assets**

In some circumstances, assets may be donated to a firm. For example, to stimulate investment in a depressed area, a local council may donate land to firms which commence operations in the area. Under these circumstances, the donated assets belong to the firm's assets. When the plant and equipment is acquired as a donation, the cost of the plant and equipment is equal to its fair market value.

(4) **Self-Constructed Assets**

Many assets are constructed by the owner rather than acquired by purchase or exchange.

The cost of self-constructed assets is the money amounts of resources embodied in the asset.

The amount of direct materials, direct labor, and variable overheads is clearly part of the cost of constructing assets and there is no dispute about their inclusion in the amount. Interest cost incurred during the construction period is viewed as part of the cost of the asset.

6.1.3 Depreciation

A business entity will often incur expenditures to acquire long-term assets for operational purposes. These expenditures can be viewed as long-term prepayments of expenses. As the assets are used for their intended purposes, utility decreases. There should be a systematic and periodic allocation of the cost associated with the acquisition of assets that corresponds to the decrease in utility and matches expenses with revenue. This cost allocation process is depreciation. Depreciation is the accounting process of allocating the periodic expiration of capital assets against the periodic revenue earned.

(1) Factors Affecting Depreciation

Four factors that influence depreciation are cost of the asset, estimated residual value (or salvage value), estimated service life, and depreciation methods.

① **The cost of the asset** is determined by the cash or cash-equivalent price paid to acquire the asset. There may be many cost components incurred to acquire and prepare the asset for its intended use.

② **The estimated residual value of the asset** is an estimate of the net realizable value of the asset to an enterprise at the end of the asset's estimated service life.

③ **The estimated service life of the asset** is the number of years that the asset economically is capable of performing its intended service.

④ **Depreciation methods** include three methods of depreciation, that is Straight-line Method, Units-of-Production Method and Accelerated Methods.

(2) Depreciation Methods

The most common methods of depreciation are the straight-line method; the units-of-production method and accelerated methods.

① **Straight-Line Method**

The straight-line method of depreciation allocates equal amounts of the cost of an asset to each accounting period during its estimated life. This method is the most common method used to allocate the cost of property, plant and equipment among accounting periods because it is easy and simple to calculate. A typical example would be depreciation for a building or for office furniture. The depreciation is computed as follows:

$$\text{Depreciation per year} = \frac{\text{Cost} - \text{Estimated Residual Value}}{\text{Service Life in Years}}$$

【Transaction 6-3】

ABC company recently purchased machinery for use purposes. Data concerning the purchase of the machinery are:

  Cost of machinery $100,000
  Estimated useful life   4 years
  Estimated residual value $10,000

Under the straight-line method, the depreciation, the depreciation expense for each year of the machinery is computed as follows:

    ($100,000 - $10,000) ÷ 4 years = $22,500 per year

The asset is decreased and owner's equity is decreased by an expense. Actual practice uses a contra-asset account called accumulated depreciation instead of long-term asset. The entry to record this depreciation expense would be:

Dec. 31	Depreciation Expense	22,500	
	Accumulated Depreciation		22,500
	To record the plant asset's depreciation expense.		

On the balance sheet, accumulated depreciation is deducted from the cost of property, plant, and equipment, and the difference called the book value (property, plant and equipment) is included in total assets.

② **Units-of-Production Method**

The units-of-production method allocates the cost of an asset to usage rather than years. This method amortizes the cost of the asset over the estimated service life as measured by estimated units of production, not by estimated years. If the use of the asset varies and the contribution to revenue differs from period to period, the units-of-production method may be appropriate. The depreciation per unit of production is determined as follows:

$$\text{Depreciation cost per unit} = \frac{\text{Cost} - \text{Estimated Residual Value}}{\text{Estimated Units of Production}}$$

Depreciation expense for period = Depreciation cost per unit × Actual production amount during current period

Note that the straight-line method provides a constant depreciation amount per year, but the units-of-production method provides a constant amount per unit of production.

【Transaction 6-4】

Using the data provided in Transaction 6-3, it is estimated that the productive life of the machinery is about 30,000 hours. If the machinery is used for 4,000 hours the first year, the depreciation expense would be:

$$\text{Depreciation cost per unit} = \frac{(\$100,000 - \$10,000) \times 4,000}{30,000} = \$12,000$$

③ **Accelerated Methods**

Accelerated methods charge higher amounts of depreciation to the earlier years of an asset's life. As an asset has greater economic benefit in the earlier years of its life than in the later years, depreciation should be allocated more in the early years of the asset's life, and the amount of depreciation charged period declines with time. An increase in repairs and maintenance costs and a decrease in revenue-producing ability in the later years of an asset's useful life suggest that accelerated methods better match revenues and expenses. Two common methods for allocating depreciation on an accelerated basis are declining-balance method and sum-of-the-year's-digits method.

a. **Declining-Balance Method**

The declining-balance method should be used for assets that are expected to benefit earlier periods of the asset's useful life more than later periods. The most common version of the declining-balance method is the double-declining-balance (DDB) method. The DDB rate is twice the rate used for the straight-line method and is calculated as:

$$DDB = \frac{2}{N}$$

N = useful life in years

Depreciation expense is calculated as follows:

Depreciation expense = DDB rate × Book value
= DDB rate × cost of asset-accumulated depreciation

Book Value represents the cost of the asset minus the accumulated depreciation. It declines at a faster rate during the early years of the asset when using the double-declining-balance method than it does using the straight-line method in each accounting period. It ignores estimated salvage when computing depreciation. The amount of depreciation calculated (twice the straight-line rate book value) may have to be adjusted in the last two periods so as not to amortize the asset beyond its residual value.

【Transaction 6-5】

Using the data provided in Transaction 6-3, under the double-declining-balance method, the depreciation cost for each accounting period is shown below:

	Deprecation Expense	Accumulated Deprecation	Net Book Value
Year 1	$ 50,000	$ 50,000	$ 50,000
Year 2	25,000	75,000	25,000
Year 3	7,500①	82,500	17,500
Year 4	7,500	90,000	10,000

Notes: DDB rate: $2/N = 2/4 = 50\%$
①: ($25,000 - $10,000)/2 = $7,500

b. Sum-of-the-Year's-Digits Method (SYD)

The sum-of-the-year's-digits method results in a decreasing depreciation expense based on a decreasing fraction of depreciable cost (original cost less residual value). Each fraction uses the sum of the years as a denominator and the number of years of estimated life remaining as of the beginning of the year as a numerator. It calculates depreciation expense by applying a rate to the asset's depreciable amount. The rate is determined by using the following formulas:

Annual depreciation expense = (cost − residual amount) × SYD rate

$$SYD\ rate = \frac{Number\ of\ Year\ of\ Useful\ Life\ at\ Beginning\ of\ Vear}{The\ Sum\ of\ the\ Year's\ Digits}$$

In this method, the numerator decreases year by year and the denominator remains constant. At the end of the asset's useful life, the balance remaining should be equal to the residual value.

【Transaction 6-6】

Use the data provided in Transaction 6-3, under the sum-of-the-year's digits method, the depreciation cost for each accounting period is shown below:

	Depreciation Fraction	Depreciation Expense	Accumulated Depredation	Net Book Value
Year 1	4/10	$36,000	$36,000	$64,000
Year 2	3/10	27,000	63,000	37,000
Year 3	2/10	18,000	81,000	19,000
Year 4	1/10	9,000	9,000	10,000

6.2 Intangible Assets

Intangible assets are assets that are used in the operation of the business but have no physical substance. Intangible assets may fall into two categories: intangible assets with limited useful lives and intangible assets with indefinite useful lives. Various intangible assets are described as follows:

(1) Patents

Patents are granted by the government, and convey the exclusive right to use a product or process for a period of certain years.

(2) Copyrights

Copyrights are also granted by the government, and convey the exclusive right to use artistic or literary works for a period of certain years beyond the author's death. Common examples of works that can be copyrighted include books, songs, and movies. The economic life of a copyright may be considerably shorter than its legal life.

(3) Trademarks

Trademarks are words, symbols, or other distinctive elements used to identify a particular firm's products.

(4) Franchises and licenses

Franchises and licenses are rights to market a particular product or service or to engage in a particular activity. For example, Pizza Hut sells franchises to various individuals and businesses. A franchise permits the holder to operate a Pizza Hut restaurant at a specified location. This right has economic value to the holder and would be reflected as an asset.

6.2.1 Acquisition of Intangible Assets

Intangible assets may be acquired from others or by the company's own research and development. If purchased externally, intangible assets should be initially recorded at their historical cost. The cost includes the acquisition cost (purchase price) and any legal fee.

【Transaction 6-7】

A company acquired a patent for $100,000 on March 5 and the entry to record this transaction would be:

March 5	Patent	100,000	
	Cash		100,000
	To record having bought a patent for cash $100,000.		

Many firms internally develop new products, as opposed to purchasing patents from others. Because large expenditures can be made without the assurance of ultimate success, this strategy is more risky and substantial uncertainty exists regarding future economic benefits. So GAAP requires that all research and development costs be expensed immediately. Research and development costs are those incurred to generate new knowledge or to translate knowledge into a new product or process. Most countries follow the practice of immediately expensing these costs.

Special accounting rules exist for software development costs. For a given project, these costs are expensed until technological feasibility is demonstrated, and costs incurred after that point are capitalized.

6.2.2 Amortization of Intangible Assets

The term amortization is used to describe the write-off expense of the cost of an intangible asset over its useful life.

The amortization of limited useful-life intangible assets is essentially the same process as the depreciation of tangible assets. It also needs to consider the useful life of assets and amortization method.

Suppose the useful life is limited by agreement or by law (e.g. 10 years for a patent), the amortization period cannot be longer. It may be shorter if the company believes that because of technological advances or other reasons, the practical life will be shorter than the legal life.

The method of amortization should reflect the pattern in which the economic benefits of the intangible asset are consumed or otherwise used up. However, if that pattern cannot be reliably determined, a straight-line amortization method will be used. Also, amortization of an intangible asset is usually credited directly to the intangible asset account rather than being accumulated in a separate contra-asset account, as is the case with accumulated depreciation.

【Transaction 6-8】

The entry recording one year's amortization of a 10-year non-renewable license that originally cost $10,000 would be:

Dec. 31	Amortization Expense	1,000	
	Licenses		1,000
	To record the amortization expense of the intangible assets.		

Intangibles assets with indefinite useful lives, such as a renewable broadcasting license, are not amortized. Rather, they are subjected to periodic impairment tests. If it is determined that such an intangible asset is impaired, its carrying value is written down to its realizable value and a charge equal to the write-down is made to income.

6.2.3　Goodwill

Goodwill is an intangible asset associated with the purchase of one company by another. Therefore, the goodwill cannot be identified because of its nature.

When one company buys another company, the purchasing company may pay more for the acquired company than the fair value of its net identifiable assets. The amount by which the purchase price exceeds the fair value of the net assets is recorded as an asset of the acquiring company.

It is important to note that goodwill arises only as part of a purchase transaction. The buying company may be willing to pay more than the fair value of the acquired net assets other than goodwill because the acquired company has a strong management team, a favorable reputation in the marketplace, superior production methods, or other unidentifiable intangible things. The acquisition cost of the recognized assets other than goodwill is their fair value at the time of acquisition. Usually, these values are determined by appraisal.

Goodwill cannot be amortized under any circumstances. It must be subjected to an annual impairment test. Any write-down due to impairment is charged to income.

6.2.4　Natural Resources and Depletion

Natural resources are recorded in the books at their cost of acquisition. The process of expense recognition for using natural resources is called depletion. The units-of-production is the most common method used to allocation the cost of natural resources.

Suppose, a mining company bought a new mine in 2018 for $13,400, plus real estate fees of $600, so total to $14,000. No salvage value is expected. The mine has approximately 28,000 tons of coal. So the cost per ton is $0.5 (i.e. 14,000 tons/ $28,000). If the company extracts 8,000 tons in the first year, the depletion cost is $4,000 (i.e. 8,000/ $0.5). The depletion of a natural resource has the same effects on the accounting equation: assets (i.e. Coal Mine) and equity (by increasing Depletion Expense) decrease. The journal entries are shown below:

Date	Account titles	Debit	Credit
1	Coal Mine	14,000	
	Cash		14,000
2	Depletion Expense	4,000	
	Coal Mine		4,000

To show the decrease in assets, a contra asset account tiled Allowance for Depletion could have been used instead of directly affecting the Coal Mine account. In such a case, Allowance for Depletion has the same relationship with natural recourses as Accumulated

Depreciation has with property, plant and equipment.

Key Words and Expressions

1. tangible asset — 有形资产
2. intangible asset — 无形资产
3. freight — 货物，运费
4. proceeds — 收入，收益
5. accumulated depreciation — 累计折旧
6. donate — 捐赠
7. direct materials — 直接材料
8. direct labor — 直接人工
9. overhead — 间接费用，制造费用
10. variable overhead — 变动间接费用
11. residual value (or salvage value) — 残值
12. units-of-production (output) method — 工作量法
13. accelerated method — 加速折旧法
14. declining-balance method — 余额递减法
15. double-declining-balance (DDB) method — 双倍余额递减法
16. sum-of-the-years-digits method — 年数总和法
17. copyright — 版权
18. trademark — 商标
19. franchises and licenses — 经营权
20. research and development — 研究开发
21. amortization — 摊销
22. amortization expense — 摊销费用
23. goodwill — 商誉
24. depletion — 损耗，(自然资源的)折损
25. patent — 专利权

Exercises

Case 1

At the beginning of year 1, a business buys a machine for $21,000 cash.

It is estimated that the machine will be used for 3 years, when it will have no scrap value under straight-line method.

Required

(1) Calculate the depreciation expense to be charged to the Profit & Loss Account for year 1.

(2) Calculate the Net Book Value to be shown on the Balance Sheet at the end of

Year 1.

(3) Calculate the depreciation expense to be charged to the Profit & Loss Account for year 2.

(4) Calculate the total depreciation provision accumulated to date as at the end of Year 2.

(5) Calculate the Net Book Value to be shown on the Balance Sheet at the end of Year 2.

(6) Calculate the depreciation expense to be charged to the Profit & Loss Account for year 3.

(7) Calculate the depreciation provision accumulated to date as at the end of Year 3.

(8) Calculate the Net Book Value to be shown on the Balance Sheet at the end of Year 3.

Case 2

Suppose a company has acquired a trademark for $10,000 that is expected to have a useful life of 5 years, and the legal life of 7 years. The annual charge is therefore $2,000 since the shorter period of 5 and 7 is 5 years and $10,000/5 years=$2,000.

Required

(1) Explain the effect of the purchase and expense recognition for the first year.

(2) Make the journal entries of purchase and expense recognition.

Extended Reading

Research and Development (R & D)

Accounting Treatment of R & D

Under International Accounting Standards the accounting for R & D is dealt with under IAS 38, Intangible Assets. IAS 38 states that an intangible asset is to be recognised if, and only if, the following criteria are met: it is probable that future economic benefits from the asset will flow to the entity; the cost of the asset can be reliably measured.

The above recognition criteria look straightforward enough, but in reality it can prove to be very difficult to assess whether or not these have been met. In order to make this recognition of intangibles more clear, IAS 38 separates an R & D project into a research phase and a development phase.

Research Phase

It is impossible to demonstrate whether or not a product or service at the research stage will generate any probable future economic benefit. As a result, IAS 38 states that all expenditure incurred at the research stage should be written off to the statement of comprehensive income as an expense when incurred, and will never be capitalised as an intangible asset.

Development Phase

Under IAS 38, an intangible asset arising from development must be capitalised if an entity can demonstrate all of the following criteria: the technical feasibility of completing the intangible asset (so that it will be available for use or sale); intention to complete and use or sell the asset; ability to use or sell the asset; existence of a market or, if to be used internally, the usefulness of the asset; availability of adequate technical, financial, and other resources to complete the asset; the cost of the asset that can be measured reliably. If any of the recognition criteria are not met then the expenditure must be charged to the income statement as incurred. Note that if the recognition criteria have been met, capitalization must take place. Once development costs have been capitalized, the asset should be amortized in accordance with the accruals concept over its finite life. Amortization must only begin when commercial production has commenced.

Questions:
(1) Outline the criteria of recognition of intangible assets.
(2) Identify the accounting treatment of research phase.
(3) Identify the accounting treatment of development phase.

Unit 7
Liabilities

Learning Objectives

After studying this unit, you should be able to:
1. Define and classify current liabilities;
2. Account for current liabilities;
3. Define and classify long-term liabilities;
4. Account for long-term liabilities.

A liability is an obligation of the business that it must eventually discharge or repay. Liabilities are what the business owes outside or external to the business.

These are two classifications of liabilities: current liabilities and non-current liabilities.

Liabilities are listed on the balance sheet based on current liabilities and long-term liabilities.

7.1 Current Liabilities

Current liabilities are obligations that the business is required to satisfy or pay within the next 12 month. An example of a current liability is:

(1) Trade creditors, which is the name we give to amounts owed to suppliers;

(2) Accruals which is the name we give to amounts still owed at the year end and not yet recorded in the books of account;

(3) Proposed items such as Dividends proposed, which means amounts the business Promises to pay in the coming year;

(4) Payable items such as tax payable which is payable within the coming year;

(5) Overdraft, which is amounts owed to the bank;

(6) Short-term loans.

Among the most common examples of current liabilities are accounts payable, short-term notes payable, the current portion of long-term debt, accrued liabilities, and unearned revenue.

7.1.1 Accounts Payable

Accounts payable, which includes details of all the amounts of money owed by the business to suppliers from whom it has purchased goods or services, with the expectation that it will pay the money owing for that purchase within the next month or two. The accounts payable include amounts owing to suppliers for inventory or stock purchased for resale, as well as amounts owing for expenses incurred or acquired by the business, such as electricity, telephone, postage and stationery. The word 'creditors' means the same as "accounts payable". Accounts payable usually do not require the payment of interest. This makes the form of liability very desirable, and it represents an "interest-free" loan from the supplier.

【Transaction 7-1】

Assume that ABC company bought office equipment for $10,000 on credit on May 15. The journal entry for this transaction was as follows:

May 15	Office Equipment (Fixed Asset)	10,000	
	Accounts Payable		10,000
	The record having bought the office equipment on credit for $10,000.		

7.1.2 Short-term Notes Payable

Short-term notes payable are issued whenever bank loans are obtained. Other transactions which may give rise to Short-term notes payable include the purchase of real estate or costly equipment, the purchase of merchandise, and the substitution of a note for a past-due account payable.

Short-term notes payable usually require the borrower to pay an interest charge. Normally, the interest rate is stated separately from the principal amount of the note.

【Transaction 7-2】

Assume that on October 1, ABC Company borrowed $100,000 from its bank for a period of three months at an annual interest rate of 10%. Six months later, on March 1, ABC Company would have to pay the bank the principal amount of $100,000 plus $5,000 interest. As evidence of this loan, the bank would require ABC Company to issue a note payable. The journal entry in ABC Company's accounting records for this October 1 borrowing was as follows:

October 1	Cash	100,000	
	Short-term notes Payable		100,000
	To record having borrowed $100,000 for three months at 10% interest per year.		

Notice that no liability was recorded for the interest charges when the note was issued. At the date that money was borrowed, the borrower had a liability only for the principal amount of the loan; the liability for the interest accrued day by day over the life of the loan. At December 31, three months' interest expense had been incurred, and the following year-end adjusting entry was made:

December 31	Interest Expense	2,500	
	Interest Payable		2,500
	To record interest expense incurred through year-end on 10% six-month.		

The entry to record payment of the note on April 1 would be:

April 1	Notes Payable	100,000	
	Interest Payable	2,500	
	Interest Expense	2,500	
	Cash		105,000
	To record payment of 10%, six-month note on maturity.		

7.1.3 The Current Portion of Long-term Debt

Some long-term debts, such as mortgage loans, are payable in a series of monthly or quarterly installments. In these cases, the principal amount due within one year (or the operating cycle) is regarded as a current liability, and the remainder of the obligation is classified as a long-term liability.

As the maturity date of a long-term liability approaches, the obligation eventually becomes due within the current period. Long-term liabilities which become payable within the coming year are reclassified in the balance sheet as current liabilities. Changing the classification of a liability does not require a journal entry; the obligation merely is shown in a different section of the balance sheet.

7.1.4 Accrued Liabilities

Accrued liabilities arise from the recognition of expenses for which payment will be made in a future period. Thus, accrued liabilities are also called accrued expenses. The need to record accrued liabilities arises from the fact that certain expenses are incurred by the business before they are actually paid. Examples of accrued liabilities include interest payable, income taxes payable, and amounts related to payrolls.

(1) Income Taxes Payable

The income taxes expense accrues as profits are earned. At the end of each accounting period, the amount of accrued income taxes is estimated and recorded in an adjusting entry, as shown below:

Dec. 31	Income Taxes Expense	72,750	
	Income Taxes Payable		72,750
	To accrue estimated income taxes expense at the end of the year.		

The account debited in the entry Income Taxes Expense is an expense account that usually appears as the very last deduction in the income statement. The liability account, Income Taxes Payable, ordinarily will be paid within a few months and, therefore, appears as a current liability section of the balance sheet.

(2) Amounts Related to Payrolls

Every business incurs a number of accrued liabilities relating to its payroll. The largest of these liabilities is the obligation to pay employees for services rendered during the period. Salaries expense is often among the largest expenses of a business organization. Accrued payroll liabilities, however, seldom accumulate to large amounts because they are paid in full at frequent intervals.

【Transaction 7-3】

To reflect salaries paid to employees $18,000 for service rendered but not yet paid for on June 30:

June 30	Salaries Expense	18,000	
	Salaries Payable		18,000
	To record this month's expense $18,000.		

7.1.5 Unearned Revenue

A liability for unearned revenue arises when a customer pays in advance. Upon receipt of an advance payment from a customer, the company debits cash and credits a liability account such as Unearned Revenue, or customers' Deposits. As the services are rendered to the customer, an entry is made debiting the liability account and crediting a revenue account. Notice that the liability for unearned revenue normally is "paid" by rendering services to the creditor, rather than by making cash payments.

【Transaction 7-4】

On December 1, 2017, assume that ABC Company collected in advance $12,000 from a customer for the service to be completed on January 31, 2018. On December 1, 2017. the journal entry to record this transaction in the cash receipts was as follows:

December 1	Cash	12,000	
	Advances on Service Revenue		12,000
	To record having received cash in advance for service $12,000.		

7.1.6 Estimated Liabilities

The term estimated liabilities refers to liabilities which appear in financial statements at estimated dollar amounts. A common example of estimated liabilities is the warranty of a product. By definition, estimated liabilities involve some degree of uncertainty. However, the liabilities are (1) known to exist, and (2) the uncertainty is not so great as to prevent the company from making a reasonable estimate and recording the liability.

7.1.7 Loss Contingencies

Loss contingencies are similar to estimated liabilities, but may involve much more uncertainty. A loss contingency is a possible loss (or expense), stemming from past events, that will be resolved as to existence and amount by some future event. A common example of a loss contingency is a lawsuit pending against a company. The lawsuit is based upon past events, but until the suit is resolved, uncertainty exists as to the amount (if any) of the company's liability.

7.2 • Long-term Liabilities

Long-term liabilities are companies' obligations that extend beyond the current year, or alternately, beyond the current operating cycle. Most commonly, these include long-term debts such as company-issued bonds.

The most common examples of long-term liabilities are long-term notes payable, bond payable and mortgage payable. Long-term financing by issuing notes payable to banks or to insurance companies can provide corporations with only a limited amount of funds.

7.2.1 Long-Term Notes Payable

A borrower may desire a longer term for their loan. It would not be uncommon to find two, three, or five-year, and even longer-term notes. These notes may evidence a "long-term loan", where "interest only" is paid during the period of borrowing, and balance of the notes are due at maturity date.

7.2.2 Bonds Payable

Bonds represent an obligation to repay a principal amount at a future date and pay interest, usually on a semi-annual basis. Unlike notes payable, which normally represent an amount owed to one lender, a large number of bonds are normally issued at the same time to different lenders. These lenders, also known as investors, may sell their bonds to another investor prior to their maturity.

(1) Bonds Issued at Par

Accounting for bonds payable closely parallels accounting for notes payable. The events in the life of a bond issue usually are:

① issuance of the bonds;

② semi-annual interest payment;

③ accrual of interest payable at the end of each accounting period; and

④ retirement of the bonds at maturity.

【Transaction 7-5】

Assume that on March 1, 2017, ABC Company issued $1,000,000 of 12%, 10-year bonds payable. These bonds were dated March 1, 2017, and interest was computed from this date. Interest on the bonds was payable semi-annually, each September 1 and March 1. If all the bonds were sold at par, they could be recorded by the following entry:

March 1	Cash	1,000,000	
	Bonds Payable		1,000,000
	To record having issued 12% 10 years bonds payable at a price of $100.		

Every September 1, during the life of the bond issue, ABC company must pay $60,000 to the bondholders. This semi-annual interest payment will be recorded as follows:

September 1	Bond Interest Expense	60,000	
	Cash		60,000
	To record semi-annual payment of bond interest.		

Every December 31, ABC company must make an adjusting entry to record the four months' interest which has accrued since September 1 as follows:

Bond Interest Expense $= 1,000,000 \times 12\% \div 12 \times 4 = 40,000$

December 31	Bond Interest Expense	40,000	
	Bond Interest Payable		40,000
	To accrue bond interest payable for four months ended on Dec. 31.		

Note that the accrued liability for bond interest payable is classified as a current liability.

Two months later, on March 1, a semi-annual interest payment is made to bondholders. The entry to record the semi-annual payments every March 1 will be:

March 1	Bonds Interest Expense	20,000	
	Bond Interest Payable	40,000	
	Cash		60,000
	To record semi-annual interest payment to recognize two months' interest expense accrued since year-end.		

When the bonds mature 10 years later on March 1, 2027, two entries are required: one entry to record the semi-annual interest payment and a second entry to record the retirement of the bonds. The entry to record retirement of the bond issue is:

March 1	Bond Payable	1,000,000	
	Cash		1,000,000
	To record having paid face amount of bond at maturity		

(2) Bonds Issued at a Discount

There is always some delay between the time a bond's coupon rate is decided upon and when the bond is actually available to be issued to the public. During this delay, the prevailing rate of return on bonds of comparable risk may have changed.

When the coupon rate is below the market rate, the investor won't buy the bonds unless they are sold at a discount from the par or face value. Because the coupon rate does not provide the investor with a rate of return equal to that available on other similar investments.

【Transaction 7-6】

Assume that on January 1, 2014, ABC Company sold $1,000,000 of 12%, 10-year bonds to an underwriter at a price of $98. On January 1, 2017, ABC Company received $980,000 cash from the underwriter and recorded a liability in this amount. But when these bonds mature in 10 years, the ABC Company will owe its bondholders $1,000,000.

Thus, the company's liabilities to bondholders will increase by $20,000 over the life of the bond issue.

When bonds are issued, the amount of any discount is debited to an account entitled Discount on Bonds Payable. Thus ABC Company will record the issuance of these bonds as follows:

January 1	Cash	980,000	
	Discount on Bonds Payable	20,000	
	Bonds Payable		1,000,000
	To record having issued $1,000,000 face value 10-year bonds to an underwriter at a price of $98.		

The debit balance account, Discount on Bonds Payable, is a contra-liability account. Over the 10-year life of the bond issue, adjusting entries are made to gradually transfer the balance in the Discount account into interest expense. Thus, the balance in the Discount account gradually declines, and the carrying value of the bonds-face value less the unamortized discount-rises toward the bonds' maturity value. At the end of each year, ABC Company will make the following adjusting entry to amortize the bond discount: amortization of discount=20,000/10=2,000

Dec. 31	Interest Expense	2,000	
	Discount on Bonds Payable		2,000
	Recognized one year's amortization of discount.		

Notice that amortization of the discount increases ABC company annual interest expense. It does not, however, require any immediate cash outlay. The interest expense represented by the discount will not be paid until the bonds mature.

(3) Bonds Issued at a Premium

When bonds are issued at a premium, the borrower pays back less than the amount originally borrowed. As a result, the total interest cost over the life of the bonds is equal to the interest paid minus the amount of the premium.

【Transaction 7-7】

Assume that on January 1 the ABC company issued $1,000,000, 12%, 10-year bonds at a price of $104. The entry to record the issuance of the bonds would be as follows:

January 1	Cash	1,040,000	
	Bonds Payable		1,000,000
	Premium on Bonds Payable		40,000
	To record having issued $1,000,000 face value 12%, 10-year bonds at a price of $104.		

The amount of any unamortized premium is added to the maturity value of the bonds payable to show the current carrying value of the liability. Over the life of the bond issue, this carrying value will be reduced toward the maturity value of $1,000,000 as the premium is amortized.

Premium is amortized in the 10-year life of the bonds in a manner similar to the amortization of discount. However, instead of increasing interest expense, amortization of premium decreases interest expense. The entry to amortize bond premium for one year is illustrated below:

Dec. 31	Premium on Bonds Payable	4,000	
	Interest Expense		4,000
	Recognized one year's amortization of premium (40,000/10=4,000) on 10-year bonds payable.		

7.2.3 Mortgage Payable

The long-term financing used to purchase property is called a mortgage. The property itself serves as collateral for the mortgage until it is paid off. A mortgage usually requires equal payments, consisting of principal and interest, throughout its term. The early payments consist of more interest than principal. Over the life of the mortgage, the portion of each payment that represents principal increases and the interest portion decreases. This decrease occurs because interest is calculated on the outstanding principal balance that declines as payments are made.

Key Words and Expressions

1. accrued liabilities　　　　　　应计负债
2. trade accounts payable　　　　应付商业账款
3. interest free　　　　　　　　　无息
4. real estate　　　　　　　　　　房地产，不动产
5. principal　　　　　　　　　　　本金
6. installment　　　　　　　　　　分期付款
7. income taxes payable　　　　　应付所得税
8. payroll　　　　　　　　　　　　工资总支出；工资名单
9. estimated liabilities　　　　　　估计负债
10. warranty　　　　　　　　　　　保证书，保修单
11. mortgage payable　　　　　　应付抵押款
12. face value　　　　　　　　　　（邮票、钱币、票等的）面值，票面价值
13. par value　　　　　　　　　　（股票的）面值，票面价值
14. coupon　　　　　　　　　　　息票
15. coupon rate　　　　　　　　　息票利率

16. nominal interest rate 名义利率
17. discount on bonds payable 应付债券折价
18. underwriter 证券代销商
19. carrying value 账面价值，置存价值
20. premium 溢价
21. premium on bonds payable 应付债券溢价

Exercises

Case 1

KFC Corporation issued $10 million of 10-year, 10% bonds on July 1, 2009, at $98.5. Interest is due on June 30 and December 31 of each year, and the bonds mature on June 30, 2019. The fiscal year ends on December 31; bond discount is amortized by the straight-line method. Prepare the following journal entries:

(1) July 1, 2009, to record the issuance of the bonds.

(2) December 31, 2009, to pay interest and amortize the bond discount.

(3) June 30, 2019, to pay interest, amortize the bond discount, and retire bonds at maturity.

Case 2

John's company issues bonds on January 1, 2017, with a principal amount of $500,000, to be repaid in 5 years and a 12% coupon rate of interest payable semiannually.

Required

(1) If the market interest rate is more than the coupon rate of 12%, when the bonds are issued, the issued price is $482,000. Prepare journal entry to record issued bonds, the payment of bonds interest and amortization of bond discount on the first interest date (July 1, 2017), and at the maturity date of company redemption of the bonds.

(2) If the market interest rate is below the coupon rate of 12%, when the bonds are issued, the issud price is $518,000. Prepare journal entry to record issued bonds, the payment of bonds interest and amortization of bond premium on the first interest date (July 1, 2017), and at the maturity date of company redemption of the bonds.

Extended Reading

Payment to Employees

A company with small number of employees may pay them with checks drawn on the firm's regular bank account. With a large number of employees, it is usually more practical to establish a separate bank account to pay the payroll.

When a company uses a separate payroll bank account, each pay period it draws a check on its regular bank account in an amount equal to the total net earnings of the employees. This check is deposited in the payroll bank account. Individual payroll checks are then drawn on this account and delivered to the employees. The issuance of the payroll checks reduces the book balance in the payroll bank account to zero.

One advantage of maintaining a separate payroll bank account is that it readily permits a division of work between the preparation and issuance of regular company checks and payroll checks. A related advantage is that it simplifies the monthly reconciliation of the regular bank account. The large number of payroll checks, many of which may be outstanding at month-end, are not run through the regular bank account. Of course, the payroll bank account also needs to be reconciled, but typically, the only reconciling item for this bank account will be payroll checks outstanding.

Sometimes employees are paid in currency and coin rather than by check. This may happen, for example, if the employees work in a location where it may not be convenient for them to deposit or cash checks. The company will prepare and cash one of its own checks for the payroll amount. Each employee's pay is put into a pay envelope and delivered to the employee. As a feature of internal control and to have evidence of the payment made, an employee should sign a receipt for the payroll envelope.

Unit 8
Owner's Equity

Learning Objectives

After studying this unit, you should be able to:
1. Understand preferred stock, and common stock;
2. Measure the effect of issuing stock on a company's financial position;
3. Account for dividends and measure their impact on a company;
4. Understand different values of a stock;
5. Report stockholders' equity transactions on the Cash Flow Statements.

The owners' equity is what the owners have put into or invested in the business; it is what the business is worth. It is an internal liability, as it shows what the business owes to the owner. The words "proprietorship" or "equity" mean the same as "owners' equity". Examples of owners' equity are:

Capital, which shows the amount and details of what has been invested by the owner in the business. Any profit made by the business is added to this capital amount. Any loss incurred by the business is deducted from the capital amount.

Drawings, which includes amounts of cash taken by the owner as well as the value of any inventory taken by the owner which the business had originally purchased to sell to its customers.

Owners' equity is a broader term because the concepts being presented are equally applicable to the ownership equity in single proprietorships, partnerships, and corporations. In this unit, accounting for partnerships will be not introduced.

8.1 Accounting for Single Proprietorship

For a single proprietorship, the owner's equity is represented by the term capital. The total capital comes from the owner's initial investment and net income. The net income is the excess of revenue over expenses for the accounting period and it is the increase in capital resulting from profitable operation of a business.

A single proprietorship is not required to maintain a distinction between invested capital and earned capital. Consequently, the balance sheet of a single proprietorship will have only one item in the owner's equity section, as illustrated below:

The owners' equity:

$$\text{Eastern Man, Capital } \$10,000$$

The distribution of cash for a single proprietorship takes the form of personal withdrawals, and a drawing account is used to show the decrease in capital. In single proprietorship, all owners' equity transactions are recorded in only two accounts: Capital and Drawings.

【Transaction 8-1】

Assume that Eastern Man decided to start a small, independent accounting firm. On January 1, 2017, he deposited $10,000 into a bank account to finance the firm. The entry to record the $10,000 deposit was:

January 1	Cash	10,000	
	Eastern Man, Capital		10,000
	To record having invested $10,000 to start an accounting Firm.		

【Transaction 8-2】

If Eastern Man decided to withdraw $500 cash for personal use or as salary on April 30, the entry was:

April 30	Eastern Man, Drawings	500	
	Cash		500
	To record having withdrawn $500 for personal use.		

8.2 Accounting for Corporation

Ownership in a corporation is evidenced by a stock certificate. This capital stock may be either common stock or preferred stock.

8.2.1 Common Stock

Common stock represents the basic ownership class of stock for a corporation. It possesses the traditional rights of ownership:

① voting rights;

② participation in dividends;

③ a residual claim to assets in the event of liquidation; and

④ preemptive right to purchase additional shares of capital stock in proportion to present holdings in the event that the corporation increases the amount of stock outstanding.

A share of stock represents a unit of the stockholders' interest in the business. The par value of a stock represents the legal capital per share. It bears no relation to the market value, that is, the current purchase or selling price. The following are several categories of stock shares.

Authorized shares are shares of stock which a corporation is permitted to issue (sell) under its articles of incorporation.

Unissued shares are authorized shares which have not yet been offered for sale.

Subscribed shares are shares which a buyer has contracted to purchase at a specific price on a certain date. The shares will not be issued until full payment has been received.

Treasury stock represents shares which have been issued and later reacquired by the corporation.

Outstanding stock represents shares authorized and issued in the hands of stockholders (Treasury stock is not outstanding, as it belongs not to the share holders but to the corporation.)

8.2.2 Preferred Stock

Preferred stock is superior to common stocks with respect to dividends, liquidation, and conversion. It is either cumulative or non-cumulative, convertible or non-convertible, depending on the agreement reached between the corporation and the preferred stockholders. Preferred stock normally possesses the following five major features:

① **Prior claim against earning.** The board of directors has the power to declare and distribute dividends to the stockholders. The claims of preferred stock are honored before those of common stock. From an accounting viewpoint, the priority in receiving dividends constitutes the most important benefit of preferred stock.

② **Prior claim to assets.** Most preferred stocks carry a preference as to assets in the event of liquidation of the corporation. If the business is terminated, the preferred stock is entitled to payment in full of its par value or a higher stated liquidation value before any payment is made on the common stock. This priority also includes any dividends in arrears.

③ **Call privilege.** The issuing company will have the right to redeem (all) the stocks at a later date for a predetermined price. This call price would be in excess of the original issue price, such as 105 percent of par value.

④ **Convertible preferred stock.** In order to add to the attractiveness of preferred stock as an investment. Corporations sometimes offer a conversion privilege which entitles the preferred stockholders to exchange their shares for common stock in a stipulated ratio.

⑤ **Cumulative preferred stock.** The dividend preference carried by most preferred stocks is a cumulative one. If all or any part of the regular dividend on the preferred stock is omitted in a given year. the amount omitted is said to be in arrears and must be paid in a subsequent year before any dividend can be paid on the common stock.

【Transaction 8-3】

ABC Corporation had outstanding 10,000 shares of preferred stocks with a preference of a $2 dividend (2 percent of $100 par value) and 5,000 shares of common stock. Net income was $30,000 and $50,000 for the first two years of operation. The board of directors had authorized the distribution of all profits.

Items	Year 1	Year 2
Net profit	$30,000	$50,000
Dividends on preferred (1000 shares, $2 per share)	$20,000	$20,000
Balance to common stock	$10,000	$30,000
Number of common stock shares	5,000	5,000
Common stock dividend per share	$2.00	$6.00

In the balance sheet, the par values or stated values of different forms of stock (preferred, common) are shown separately, as is any excess or deficiency received for the shares.

(1) Issuance of Capital Stock

The articles of the corporation specify the number of shares that a corporation is authorized to issue by the country of incorporation. Issues of capital stock that will be sold to the public must be approved by the Securities Exchange Commissions (SEC).

The numbers of shares which have been issued and are in hands of stockholders are called the outstanding shares. At any time, those outstanding shares represent 100% of the stockholders' equity in the corporation.

① **Issuing at Par Value**

Many states require that stock have a designated par value (or in some cases "stated value"). Thus, par value is said to represent the "legal capital" of the firm.

【Transaction 8-4】

Assume that on January 1, ABC Corporation was authorized to issue 1,00,000 shares of preferred stock, $5 par, and 1,000,000 shares of common stock, $1 par. The authorized shares were issued at par for cash. The entry to record the stockholders' investment and the receipt of the cash would be as follows:

January 1	Cash	1,500,000	
	Preferred Stock		500,000
	Common Stock		1,000,000
	To record the corporation issued preferred stock and common stock.		

The stock accounts (preferred stock, common stock) are controlling accounts. A record of each stockholder's name, address, and number of shares held is normally kept in a subsidiary ledger. This subsidiary ledger is called the stockholders' ledger. It provides the information for issuing dividend checks, annual meeting notices, and financial reports to individual stockholders.

② Issuing at Premium (or Discount)

When stock is issued for a price that is more than its par, the stock has sold at a premium. When stock is issued for a price that is less than its par, the stock has sold at a discount. Thus, if stock with a par of $50 is issued for a price of $60, the stock has sold at a premium of $10. If the same stock is issued for a price of $45, the stock has sold at a discount of $5. Many countries do not permit the issuance of stock at a discount. In others, it may be done only under unusual conditions. Since issuing stock at a discount is rare, we will not illustrate it.

When stock is issued at a premium, cash or other asset accounts are debited for the amount received. The stock account is then credited for the par amount. The excess of the amount paid over par is a part of the total investment of the stockholders in the corporation. Therefore, such an amount in excess of par should be classified as a part of the paid-in capital. An account entitled Additional Paid-in Capital is usually credited for this amount.

【Transaction 8-5】

Assume that on January 1, ABC Corporation issued 1,000 share of 50 par common stock for cash at $55. The entry to record the transaction would be as follows:

January 1	Cash	550,000	
	Common Stock		500,000
	Additional Paid-in Capital		50,000
	To record the corporation having issued common stock at a premium.		

(2) Dividends

A dividend is a distribution of cash (or other assets) or capital stock to shareholders by a corporation at the end of a year. Commonly, there are two kinds of dividends for a corporation: cash dividends and stock dividends.

① Cash Dividends

The payment of cash dividends must meet three requirements: retained earnings, an adequate cash position and dividend action by the board of directors. Dividends are paid only through action by the board of directors. Whatever the case, a company has no obligation to pay a dividend, and there is no "liability" for the dividend until such time as they are actually declared. A "declaration" is a formal action by the board of directors to indicate that a dividend will be paid at some stipulated future date.

【Transaction 8-6】

On the date of declaration, December 10, the following entry was needed on the Corporate accounts:

Dec. 10	Dividends Expense	50,000	
	Dividends Payable		50,000
	To record declaration of dividends on common stock (assumed $0.5 per share on 100,000 shares outstanding);		
	To be paid on Jan. 25 next year.		
Jan. 20	Dividends Payable	50,000	
	Cash		50,000
	To record payment of previously declared dividends.		

The account Dividends Payable, which was credited at the date of declaring the dividend, is a current liability. The Dividends Expense account is a "temporary" owner's equity account, similar to the owner's drawing account in a single proprietorship. A closing entry is required at the end of the year to transfer the debit balance in the Dividends account into the Retained Earning account.

【Transaction 8-7】

Assume that ABC Company had declared four quarterly dividends during the current year. Each in the amount of $100,000. The year-end entry to close the Dividends Expense account would be:

Dec. 31	Retained Earnings	400,000	
	Dividends Expense		400,000
	To close the Dividends Expense account at year-end by transferring its debit balance into the Retained Earning account.		

② Stock Dividends

In contrast to cash dividends discussed earlier, stock dividends involve the issuance of additional shares of stock to existing shareholders on a proportional basis. For example, a shareholder who owns 100 shares of stock will own shares after a 25% stock dividend. Importantly, all shareholders would have 25% more shares, so his or her percentage ownership in the corporation is no larger than before.

(3) Treasury Stock

Treasury stock is a corporation's own stock that has been issued and subsequently reacquired by purchases. Treasury stock may be purchased for a variety of reasons, including reissuing them to officers and employees in profit sharing schemes or stock-option plans. Whatever the purposes, the corporation is in reality reducing owner's capital for a period of time. It is commonly recorded at cost and shown as a deduction from total stockholders' equity in the balance sheet.

(4) The Different Values of a Stock

The market value of a stock is its current selling price. Market value is more important to stockholders than any of the other value mentioned here.

The redemption value of a stock is the price the corporation pays to buy back its preferred stock. Redeemable preferred stock is a liability, because the corporation has the obligation to redeem preferred stock at the option of the stockholder.

The book value of a stock measures the amount of net assets or stockholders' equity per share.

① Book value is based on historical cost of the net assets and is not market value.

② Common book value = (Total stockholders' equity-preferred equity) ÷ number of common shares outstanding.

③ Preferred equity = Redemption value + dividends in arrears.

8.2.3 Reporting Stockholders' Equity Transactions on the Statement of Cash Flows

Stockholders equity transactions are financing activities. These financing transactions include:

① Issuances of stock;

② Purchase of treasury stock or retirement of stock;

③ Payment of dividends.

Companies use a variety of terminology and formats in reporting stockholders' equity.

Key Words and Expressions

1. proprietorship 所有（权）
2. shareholder 股东
3. outstanding 发行在外的股份
4. preferred 优先股
5. common stock 普通股
6. issuing stock 发行股票
7. paid-in capital 缴入股本，投入股本
8. contributed capital 实缴股本
9. authorized share 法定的股份
10. unissued share 未发行的股份
11. treasury stock 库藏股

12.	cumulative	累积的
13.	board of director	董事会
14.	call privilege	优先赎回
15.	call price	赎回价格
16.	cash dividend	现金股利
17.	stock dividend	股票股利

Exercises

Case 1

ABC Company began operation in 2017. In that year, the corporation earned net income of $195,000 and paid dividends of $2.25 per share on its 40,000 outstanding shares of capital stock. In 2018, the corporation incurred a net loss of $127,000 and paid no dividends.

(1) Prepare the journal entry to close the Income Summary account 2018 (the year of the $127,000 net loss).

(2) Compute the amount of returned earnings which appear in the company's balance sheet at December 31, 2018.

(3) Has ABC Company's operation been profitable for two years according to accounting data?

Case 2

Four events pertaining to ABC Company are described below:

(1) Declared and paid a cash dividend.

(2) Issued a 20% stock dividend.

(3) Purchased treasury stock.

(4) Reissued the treasury stock at a price higher than the purchase price.

Indicate the immediate effects of the events on the financial measurements and fill in the table below, using the code letters, "I" for increase, "D" for decrease, and "NE" for no effect.

Event	Current assets	Owner's equity	Net income	Net cash flow

Case 3

ABC Corporation had the following transactions:

(1) Issued five million shares of $1 par value preferred stock at a price of $10.

(2) Purchased 100,000 shares of its common stock as treasury stock at a market price of $35.

Use the balance sheet equation to analyze the financial statement effects of these transactions and set up the following columns: cash, preferred stock, additional paid-in capital, common stock, and treasury stock.

Extended Reading

What are LEAPS and How to Trade Them

ZYX is currently trading at 50-1/2 and a ZYX LEAPS call option, and with a two-year expiration and a strike price of 50, is trading for a premium of 8 1/2, or $850 per contract. The investor buys five contracts for a total cost of $4,250. The calls give the investor the right to buy 500 shares of ZYX between now and expiration at $50 per share regardless of how high the price of the stock rises. To be profitable, though, at expiration, the stock must be trading for more than 58, the total of the option premium (8 1/2) and the strike price of 50. This is known as the breakeven point. The buyer's maximum loss for this strategy is equal to the total cost of the options, or $4,250. The following are possible outcomes of this strategy at expiration.

ZYX is trading above the breakeven point. If ZYX advances to 65 at expiration, the LEAPS will have a value of approximately 15 (the stock price of 65 less the strike price of 50). The investor may choose to exercise the calls and take delivery of the stock at a price of 50, or may sell the LEAPS calls for a profit.

Unit 9
Measurement of Bussiness Income

Learning Objectives ▶▶

After studying this unit, you should be able to:
1. Define the revenue and expenses;
2. Understand the classification of the revenue and expenses;
3. Measure the revenue and expenses;
4. Recognize the revenue and expenses.

In business, revenue is the assets increase that a company receives from its normal business activities, usually from the sales of goods and services to customers.

9.1 • Revenue

9.1.1 What is Revenue

Revenue is the earnings, proceeds or takings from the operations of a business. The word "income" means the same as "revenue". Examples of revenue are:

Sales, which includes the total amount or price obtained by the business when it sells its inventory or goods. This is the main revenue source for a business selling inventory or goods.

Fees, which includes the total amount or price obtained by the business when it sells its services. This is the main revenue source for a business selling services.

Commission received, which is revenue received from selling someone else's inventory, goods or property. It is not usually the main revenue source.

Interest received, which is revenue received from investments that the business has made with money it has had available. This may include interest-bearing deposits with a bank or other borrowing institution. It is not usually the main revenue source.

Rent received, which is revenue received from renting to a third party or portion of a building that the business owns or has available but does not need to use, and has therefore decided to earn revenue by renting it out. It is not usually the main revenue source.

9.1.2 Measurement of Revenue

Revenue should be measured at the fair value of the consideration received or receivable. The amount of revenue arising in a transaction is usually determined by the agreement between the enterprise and the buyer or user of the asset. It is measured at the fair value of the consideration received or receivable taking into account the amount of any trade discounts and volume rebates allowed by the enterprise.

In most cases, the consideration is in the form of cash or cash equivalents and the amount of revenue is the amount of cash or cash equivalents received or receivable. However, when the inflow of cash or cash equivalents is deferred, the fair value of the consideration may be less than the nominal amount of cash received or receivable. For example, an enterprise may provide interest free credit to the buyer or accept a note receivable bearing a below-market interest rate from the buyer as consideration for the sale of goods. When the arrangement effectively constitutes a financing transaction, the fair value of the consideration is determined by discounting all future receipts using an imputed rate of interest. The imputed rate of interest is more clearly determinable of either: the prevailing rate for a similar instrument of an issuer with a similar credit rating; or a rate of interest that discounts the nominal amount of the instrument to the current cash sales price of the goods or services.

When the fair value of the goods and services received cannot be measured reliably, the revenue is measured at the fair value of the goods or services given up, adjusted by the amount of any cash or cash equivalent transferred.

9.1.3 Recognition of Revenue

The generally accounting accepted principles (GAAP) determine the specific conditions under which income becomes realized as revenue. Generally, revenue is recognized only when a specific critical event has occurred and the amount of revenue is measurable.

For most businesses, income is recognized as revenue whenever the company delivers or performs its product or service and receives payment for it. Revenue recognition needs to meet the following conditions:

① Revenue is realized when cash or claims to cash (receivable) are received in exchange for goods or services.

② Revenue is realizable when assets received in such exchange are readily convertible to cash or claims to cash.

③ Revenue is earned when such goods or services are transferred (rendered). Both such payment assurance and final delivery completion (with a provision for returns, warranty claims, etc.) are required for revenue recognition.

The ways to recognize the revenue in the following four types of transactions:

① Revenues from selling goods are recognized at the date of sale often interpreted as the date of delivery.

② Revenues from rendering services are recognized when services are completed and billed.

③ Revenue from permission to use company's assets (e.g. interests for using money, rent for using fixed assets, and royalties for using intangible assets) is recognized as time passes, or as assets are used.

④ Revenue from selling an asset other than inventory is recognized at the point of sale when it takes place.

In practice, this means that revenue is recognized when an invoice has been sent.

(1) Sales

The procedures used in accounting for sales depend on several factors. A great deal depends on the types of businesses, organizations of the sales departments, types of goods sold, volume of sales, methods of selling, and the sales terms. There are a number of steps in the accounting cycle for sales transactions. When the orders are received, they must be examined for acceptability, terms determined, credit approved, a sales invoice prepared, merchandise packed and shipped or delivered, and finally collection is made before the sales cycle is completed.

① **Sales for Cash**

While some businesses sell for cash or on credit, others sell for cash only. Examples include snack shops, food stores, and some gas stations. Various procedures are used to handle cash sales and cash registers are usually employed. The cash register is a means of internal control since the total cash sales for the day should be reconciled to the cash in the register drawer.

【Transaction】

Butler Engineering received $93.50 for inventory or goods sold for cash including 10% GST on March 12.

March 12	Cash	93.50	
	Sales		85
	GST		8.5
	To record sold for cash including 10% GST.		

② **Sales on Credit**

Sales on credit are often referred to sales on account or charge sales. In such a sales transaction, the seller exchanges merchandise for the buyer's promise to pay at a later date. Most wholesale sales and a significant portion of retail sales are now made on credit. Since the business that sells on account assumes an additional risk, it is best to investigate the financial condition of the buyers. Larger businesses often have a credit department which establishes credit policies and approves or disapproves individual credit sales. Experienced credit managers have learned to establish credit policies that will neither be so tight as to reduce sales nor so loose as to create excessive bad debt losses.

(2) Trade and Cash Discounts

Manufacturers and wholesalers publish catalogs in order to describe their products and list their retail prices. Usually, they offer deductions from these list prices to dealers who buy in large quantities. These deductions are known as trade discounts. By offering these discounts, a business can adjust a price at which it is willing to bill its goods without changing the list price in the catalog. For example, ABC Company wants to advertise its stereo radio at a list price of $150. However, the radio is offered to dealers at a trade discount of 30%, which amounts to $45. Therefore, the dealer pays only $105 for the radio.

While trade discounts are used to make price differentials among different classes of customers and as a means of avoiding catalog revisions, cash discounts are used primarily to induce prompt payment by customers. In other words, the seller may allow the buyer to deduct a certain percent of the bill if he or she makes the payment before the amount is due. The payment terms should be clearly stated on the face of the invoice. The following are examples of some commonly used terms.

2/10, n/30. This is read as "two ten, net thirty" and means that a 2 percent discount of the invoice price is allowed if payment is made within 10 days following the invoice date, and the gross invoice price is due 30 days from the invoice date.

9.2 Expense

In order to earn revenue, the cost expenditure of every business will occur.

9.2.1 What is Expense

Expense is what is incurred or spent in marking the sales, and in running the business. For our purposes, 'cost' means the same as 'expense'. Examples of expense are:

Cost of goods sold, which is the cost of the goods that have been sold by the business.

Wages or salaries, which are paid to the people who work for the business—they are employees of the business.

Rent expense, which is the amount paid to another business for the right to use an area of land and/or building to store inventory and carry out the activities of the business.

Postage expense, which includes the cost of sending and receiving items through the mail, that is, Australia post.

Stationery expense, which includes the cost of pens, pencils, biros, paper and preprinted forms used by the business.

An expense always causes a decrease in owner's equity. The related changes in the accounting equation can be either (1) a decrease in assets, or (2) an increase in liabilities. An expense reduces assets if payment occurs at the time that the expense is recorded or if payment has been made in advance. If the expense will not be paid until later, as, for example, the purchase of advertising services on account, the recording of the expenses will be accompanied by an increase in liabilities.

9.2.2 Recognition of Expenses

The matching principle states that all expenses that were incurred to generate the revenue appearing on a given period's income statement should appear as an expense on the same income statement. In other words, we should match expenses against revenue. Revenue is first recognized and expenses are then matched with those revenue. Commonly, an entity shall recognize an expense when and only when (1) it is probable that the expenses have occurred, and (2) the expenses can be measured reliably.

Where an item does not satisfy the recognition criteria, and that information is material and relevant to users of the financial statements, the notes to the financial statements should disclose the item. An entity should recognize expenses for the period the entity was responsible for the relevant functions.

9.2.3 Categories of Expenses

The categories of expenses (according to their nature or type) included in this section reflect common expense categories. They are salary expenses, supplies and services, borrowing cost expenses, depreciation, loss on disposal of non-current assets, inventory expenses, bad and doubtful debts, resources provided or received free of charge, expenses related to assumed liabilities, extraordinary items and so on. The following are several simple expenses.

(1) Salary Expenses

Salary expenses are the entitlements which employees accumulate as a result of rendering their services to an employer. Salary expenses are the employing entity's own expenditure. Salary expenses should reflect the cost of staff as they provide their services on an accrual basis.

(2) Supplies Expenses

Supplies expenses include recurrent expense items such as accommodation, repairs and maintenance, minor assets not required to be capitalized, travel and associated travel costs, office requisites, postage, audit fees, computer services, legal services, consultants, telecommunication services, insurance premiums, and other supplies expenses.

(3) Borrowing Cost Expenses

Borrowing cost expenses are defined as "interest and other costs incurred by an entity in connection with the borrowing of funds".

Borrowing cost expenses include interest on bank overdrafts and short-term and long-term borrowings, amortization of discounts or premiums relating to borrowings, amortization of ancillary costs incurred in connection with the arrangements of borrowings, and finance charges in respect of finance lease recognized.

(4) Depreciation and Amortization

Depreciation (amortization) is a periodic expense of operations and is associated with the consumption or loss of service potential of non-current assets. This consumption or loss may occur through use, wear and tear, or obsolescence. Amortization is used in relation to intangible and leased assets, while depreciation is applied to physical assets such as property, plant and equipment.

(5) Inventory Expenses

Inventory expenses are the reduction in the inventory assets by way of use or loss (theft, damage or obsolescence). Where the inventory assets are entity assets, the inventory expenses are entity's expenses.

(6) Bad and Doubtful Debts Expenses

Bad and doubtful debts expenses are, in effect, reduction of the "allowance of asset". Doubtful debts expenses are an estimate of the amount of receivables outstanding at the end of the reporting period that the entity anticipates it will not recover, but has not written off as a bad debt. Bad debts expenses represent receivables that the entity has written off as uncollectible. The debtor may not be able to make payment, or the entity may have decided that it is impracticable to enforce payment.

When an entity considers it probable, it will not receive full or part payment of a receivable, and the entity shall recognize an expense as soon as it considers that the receivable will not be recovered. This may be done by writing off receivable as a bad debt or by making an allowance for a doubtful debt.

If the total sales revenue is greater than the total expenses then the business has made a profit; this is added to the owner's equity.

9.3 Business Income

Business enterprise is continuously engaged in activities aimed at earning income. It would be fairly easy to determine the income of company if we could wait until the business ceased to exist. However, the business environment required a firm to report income or loss regularly for short and equal periods of time. For example, stockholder must receive income reports every year, and the management often wants financial statement to be prepared every month.

To the accountant, net income (net loss) is the net increase (decrease) in owners' equity resulting from the operations of the company. Net income (net loss) equals the difference between revenue and expenses.

$$\boxed{\text{Net income}} = \boxed{\text{Revenue}} - \boxed{\text{Expense}}$$

For example, ABC Company buys equipment that it leases out to earn revenue. The company engaged in its first month of operation as follows. The owners of the company made only one investment to start the business and no withdrawals.

a. Buy equipment on account, $80,000
b. Perform service for cash, $1,600

c. Perform service on account, $500

d. Paid cash on account, $10,000

e. Perform service on account, $850

f. Received cash on account, $150

g. Paid cash expenses, $2,000

If these transactions fully describe the operations of ABC Company during the month, what was the amount of net income or net loss?

Revenue ($1,600 + $500 + $850) − Expense($2,000) = Net Income ($950)

Key Words and Expressions

1. inflow　　　　　　　　　流入，涌入
2. commission revenue　　　佣金收入
3. interest revenue　　　　　利息收入
4. rebate　　　　　　　　　折扣，回扣
5. imputed rate　　　　　　应计利率，推算利率
6. prevailing rate　　　　　　现时利率，现行利率
7. equivalent　　　　　　　等价物
8. cash equivalent　　　　　现金等价物
9. recognition　　　　　　　认出，识别；承认，认可
10. salary expenses　　　　　工资费用
11. borrowing cost expenses　借款成本费用
12. bad and doubtful expenses　坏账费用
13. insurance premium　　　保险费用
14. ancillary　　　　　　　　辅助的

Exercises

Case 1

Smith, a Kansas wheat farmer, harvested 100,000 bushels of wheat at the end of Year 1. The price of the wheat on that date was $4.5 per bushel. His cost of producing the wheat was $2.8 per bushel. Smith sold 140,000 bushels in Year 1 for $4.5 per bushel and stored the remainder. Two months into Year 2, the price suddenly dropped to $3.25 per bushel. Smith immediately sold the remaining wheat at $3.25.

Required

(1) Calculate the income to be recognized under the market price method for Year 1 and Year 2.

(2) Present the entry that would be necessary to report the bushels in storage at the end of Year 1.

(3) Calculate the income to be recognized under the completed transaction method for Year 1 and Year 2.

Case 2

ABC Corporation began business on Jan. 1, Year 1. The corporation properly used the installment sales method of accounting for revenue. The following information was available for Year 1 and Year 2:

	Year 1	Year 2
Gross Profit Percentage	25%	30%
Balance of Deferred Gross Profit on Installment Sales for:		
Year 1	$ 150,000	$ 60,000
Year 2		$ 240,000

Required

Calculate the balance of the installment accounts receivable at the end of Year 2.

Extended Reading

Matching Principal

The concept of matching revenues and expenses to arrive at profit or loss for a period is perhaps the most fundamental in accounting. It requires the matching against revenue of all the costs (expenses) incurred in earning that revenue regardless of when they are paid.

Expenses may be paid in advance, or sometime after they are incurred, but the accounting system must be capable of matching expenses to the revenue they help to earn, so that the resultant net profit accurately represents the results for the reporting period.

The principle relating to prepayments and accruals are also applied to the revenues for the period in the matching process

Test Your Understanding

(1) Why is it important to match revenue earned with the expenses incurred in earning those revenues?

(2) Why should non-material information be excluded from the accounting reports?

Unit 10
Financial Statements

Learning Objectives ▶▶

After studying this unit, you should be able to:
1. Understand the purpose of the financial statements;
2. Explain the format of the financial statements;
3. Understand the classification of the financial statements;
4. Explain the limitations of the financial statements.

The financial statements are the means of conveying to the management and to the interested outsiders a concise picture of the profitability and financial position of a business. The usual accounting period is one year, for which complete financial statements are prepared and distributed to investors, bankers, and governmental agencies. However, most businesses also prepare quarterly and monthly financial statements so that the management will be currently informed on the profitability and financial position of the business from month to month. The basic financial statements include the balance sheet, the income statement, the statement of owner's equity, and the statement of cash flows. Every large corporation prepares annual financial statements which are distributed to all owners of the business. In addition, these statements are filed with various governmental agencies and become a matter of public record.

10.1 Balance Sheet

The balance sheet is one of the basic financial statements. It is the main source of financial information to persons outside the business organization and is also useful to the management. They show the financial position of the business at the end of the time period and the changing results by which the business arrived at this financial position.

Every business prepares a balance sheet at the end of the year. The balance sheet may be arranged in either account form or report form.

In the account form, the assets are listed on the left side of the table and liabilities and owner's equity on the right side. And in the report form, the liabilities and owner's equity sections are listed below rather than to the right of the asset section. Both the account form and the report form are widely used. Exhibit 10-1 illustrates the account form of the balance sheet and Exhibit 10-2 illustrates the report form of the balance sheet.

Note that the balance sheet sets forth in its heading three items:

(1) the name of the business.

(2) the name of the financial statement "Balance Sheet".

(3) the date of the balance sheet.

Under the heading is the body of the balance sheet, which consists of three distinct sections: assets, liabilities and owner's equity.

Another point to note about the form of a balance sheet is that cash is always the first asset listed. It is followed by receivables, supplies, and any other assets that will soon be converted into cash or consumed in operations. Following these items are the more permanent assets, such as land, buildings and equipment. The liabilities of a business are always listed before the owner's equity.

Exhibit 10-1 Account Form of the Balance Sheet

ABC Co. LTD
Balance Sheet
Dec. 31, 2017

Assets	Amounts	Liabilities and Owner's Equity	Amounts
		Liabilities	
Cash	$ 61,500	Notes Payable	$ 78,000
Accounts Receivable	195,000	Accounts Payable	108,000
Supplies	4,500	Income Taxes Payable	54,000
Land	204,000	Total Liabilities	$ 240,000
Buildings	400,500	Owner's Equity	
Cleaning Equipment	117,000	Capital Stock	675,000
Delivery Equipment	67,500	Retained Earnings	135,000
		Total Owner's Equity	$ 810,000
Total Assets	$ 1,050,000	Total Liabilities and Owner's Equity	$ 1,050,000

Exhibit 10-2 Report Form of the Balance Sheet

ABC Co. LTD
Balance Sheet
Dec. 31, 2017

Assets

Cash ·· $ 61,500
Accounts Receivable ·· 195,000
Supplies ·· 4,500
Land ·· 204,000

Buildings	400,500
Cleaning Equipment	117,000
Delivery Equipment	67,500

Liabilities & Owner's Equity

Liabilities:

Notes Payable	$78,000
Accounts Payable	108,000
Income Taxes Payable	54,000
Total liabilities	$240,000

Owner's Equity:

Capital Stock	$675,000
Retained Earnings	135,000
Total Owner's Equity	$810,000
Total Liabilities and Owner's Equity	$1,050,000

10.2 Income Statement

An income statement is a financial statement showing the results of operations for a business by matching revenue and related expenses for a particular accounting period. It shows the net income or net loss.

There are two common forms of the income statements: the multiple-step income statement and the single-step income statement.

(1) Multiple-step Income Statement

The multiple-step income statement is so named because of the series of steps in which costs and expenses are deducted from revenue. As a first step, the cost of goods sold is subtracted from net sales to produce an amount for gross profit on sales. As a second step, operating expenses are deducted to obtain a subtotal term income from operation (or operating income). As a final step, income tax expenses are subtracted to determine net income. The multiple-step income statement is noted for its numerous sections and significant subtotals. It is also a classified income statement because the various items of expenses are classified into significant groups.

The classified income statement enables management, stockholders, analysts, and others to study the changes in the expenses over successive accounting period. The items of an income statement may be classified as the following four groups.

① **Revenue.** This includes gross income from the sale of product or services. It may be designated as Sales, Income from Fees, and so on, to indicate gross income. The gross amount is reduced by sales returns and allowances and sales discounts to net sales.

② **Cost of goods sold.** This includes the costs related to the products or services sold. It would be relatively simple to compute for a firm that retails goods; it would be more complex for a manufacturing firm that changes raw materials into finished products.

③ **Operating expenses.** This includes all expenses or resources consumed in obtaining rev-enue. Operating expenses are further divided into two groups: selling expenses, general and administrative expenses. Selling expenses are those related to the promotion and sale of the company's products or services. General and administrative expenses are those related to the overall activities of the business, such as the salaries of the president and other officers.

④ **Other expenses.** This includes non-operating and incidental expenses. Non-operating expenses may take a variety of forms. The most common type relates to interest charges or other costs of borrowing. Income tax is shown as a non-operating expense because they do not help to produce operating revenue (sales). Incidental expenses that are incurred as a result of casualty or theft, such as emergency room treatment for injury suffered as a result of mugging, are not deductible as a casualty loss. Those expenses appear in the final section of the income statement after the figure showing income from operations.

Multiple-step income statement is widely used by most businesses, and is the official format of income statement in China. Exhibit 10-3 is an illustration of the multiple-step income statement.

Exhibit 10-3 The Multiple-Step Income Statement

ABC CORPORATION

Income Statement

For the year ended December 31, 2017

Revenue:

Sales			$ 506,000
Less: Sales return and allowances		$ 4,000	
Sales discounts		2,000	6,000
Net sales			$ 50,000
Cost of goods sold			
Inventory. Dec. 1			$ 60,000
Purchases			$ 300,000
Less: Purchase returns and allowances		$ 2,000	
Purchase discounts		$ 1,000	3,000
Net purchases			$ 297,000
Add: Transportation in			13,000
Cost of goods purchased			310,000
Cost of goods available for sale			370,000
Less: Inventory Dec. 31			$ 300,000
Cost of goods sold			$ 200,000

Gross profit on sales
  Operating expenses:
    Selling expenses
    Sales salaries expenses $76,000
    Delivery service 4,000
    Advertising expenses 16,000
    Depreciation expenses 9,000
  Total selling expenses $105,000
General and administrative expenses:
    Office salaries expenses $60,000
    Telephone expenses 2,000
    Depreciation expenses 8,000
  Total general and administrative expenses 70,000
  Total operating expenses income from operations 175,000
  Income from operation $25,000
  Income tax expenses 5,000
  Net income $20,000
  Basic earnings per share $1.95

(2) Single-step Income Statement

The income statements prepared by large corporations for distribution to thousands of stockholders are often greatly condensed because the public is presumably more interested in a concise report than in the details of operation. The single-step form of income statement takes its name from the fact that the total of all expenses (including the cost of goods sold) is deducted from total revenue in a single step. All revenue, such as sales, interest earned, and rent revenue, are added together to show the total revenue. Then all expenses are grouped together and deducted in one step without the use of subtotal. A condensed income statement in single-step, form is shown below (Exhibit 10-4).

Exhibit 10-4 The Single-Step Income Statement

ABC CORPORATION

Income Statement

For the year ended December 31, 2017

Revenue:
  Net sales $90,000,000
  Interest earned 1,800,000
  Total revenue $91,800,000
Expenses:
  Cost of goods sold $60,000,000
  Selling Expenses 14,400,000
  General administrative expenses 9,750,000

Income tax expenses		3,150,000
Total expenses		$8,730,000
Net income		$4,500,000

Use of the single-step income statement has increased in recent years, perhaps because it is relatively simple and easy to read. A disadvantage of this format is that some useful items such as the gross profit on sales are not readily apparent, and they are important for the financial analysis.

10.3 The Statement of Owner's Equity

In the business, a statement of owner's equity is frequently prepared to accompany the balance sheet and income statement. This is simply a summary of the changes in the owner's capital balance during the accounting period. Exhibit 10-5 shows this type of statement for Douglas Trading Company.

Exhibit 10-5 The Statement of Owner's Equity

DOUGLAS TRADING COMPANY
Statement of Owner's Equity
For the Month Ended Jan. 31, 2017

K. Douglas. Capital—Jan. 1		$120,000
Add: Capital Contributed in Jan.	$40,000	
Net income for Jan.	36,000	76,000
		$196,000
Less: Capital Withdrawn in Jan		16,000
K. Douglas. Capital—Jan. 31		$180,000

This statement further demonstrates the relationship between the income statement and the balance sheet. The net income (or net loss) for a period in the income statement is an input into the statement of owner's equity, while the ending owner's equity balance on this statement is an input into the balance sheet at the end of the period.

However, corporations prepare a similar statement called the statement of retained earnings, which shows the beginning retained earnings, the net income and dividends for the period, and the ending retained earnings.

10.4 The Statement of Cash Flows

A statement of cash flows reports the cash receipts and cash payments of an entity during a period. It explains the causes for the changes in cash by providing information about operating, financing and investing activities.

(1) Operating Activities

Operating activities are those activities that are part of the day-to-day business of a company. Cash receipts from selling goods or from providing services are the major operating cash inflows. Major operating cash outflows include payments to purchase inventory and to pay wages, taxes, interest, utilities, rent, and similar expenses.

(2) Investing Activities

The primary investing activities are the purchase and sale of land, buildings, and equipment. You can think of investing activities as those activities associated with buying and selling long-term assets.

(3) Financing Activities

Financing activities are those activities whereby cash is obtained from or repaid to owners and creditors. For example, cash received from owners' investments. Cash proceeds from a loan or cash payments to repay loans would all be classified under financing activities.

The statement of cash flows for ABC Co. LTD for the period January 1~31, 2017 is presented in Exhibit 10-6.

Exhibit 10-6 The Statement of Cash Flows

ABC Co. LTD
Statement of Cash Flows
For the Period January 1~31, 2017

Cash flows from operating activities:

Cash received from revenue transactions	$ 2,200
Cash paid for expenses	(1,400)
Net cash provided by operating activities	<u>800</u>

Cash flows from investing activities:

Purchase of land	$ (52,000)
Purchase of buildings	(6,000)
Purchase of tools	(6,800)
Sales of tools	600
Net cash used by investing activities	<u>(64,200)</u>

Cash flows from financing activities:

Sale of capital stock	$ 80,000
Increase in cash for the period	$ 16,600
Beginning cash balance, January 1, 2017	0
Ending cash balance, January 31, 2017	$ 16,600

In common companies, positive cash flows should be generated from operations. Usually, cash from investing activities is negative, reflecting the fact that most companies are using cash to expand or enhance long-term assets. Positive cash flows from financing activities can be a sign of a young, rapidly expanding company in need of external financing. Negative cash flows from financing activities might be exhibited by a mature company.

The basic financial statements are designed to satisfy the needs of a variety of users of financial information. In analyzing a business, the users of financial statements should consider its liquidity, solvency, and profitability. Moreover, the users of financial statements should also pay more attention to the accompanying notes to financial statements.

These explanatory notes provide additional information about certain items and dollar amounts in the financial statements. They are considered as an important integral part of the financial statements.

Key Words and Expressions

1. concise — 简明的，概括的
2. the statement of owner's equity — 业主权益表，所有者权益表
3. the statement of cash flows — 现金流量表
4. account form — 账户形式，账户格式
5. report form — 报告形式，报告格式
6. convert — 转变，兑换，置换
7. permanent asset — 永久性资产，固定资产
8. economic performance — 经济成果(绩效)
9. prospective investor — 可能的投资者，潜在的投资人
10. coincide — 时间上相合
11. slack season — 淡季，萧条季节
12. multiple-step — 多步骤的，多步式的
13. single-step — 单步骤的，单步式的
14. gross profit — 毛利
15. incidental expense — 杂费，临时性费用，偶尔发生的费用
16. condensed — 缩小的，缩短的
17. the statement of retained earnings — 留存收益表
18. cash flow — 现金流量
19. operating activity — 经营活动
20. investing activity — 投资活动
21. financing activity — 筹资活动
22. positive cash flow — 正现金流量
23. negative cash flow — 负现金流量
24. liquidity — 资产流动性
25. solvency — 偿债能力

Case 1

Based on the following information, determine the capital of December 31, 2017:

Net income for the period, $18,000; Drawing, $6,000; Capital (January 1, 2017), $20,000.

Case 2

The following information was taken from an income statement: Fees Income, $14,000; Rent Expense, $2,000; Salary Expense, $5,000; Miscellaneous Expense, $1,000. If the owner withdrew $2,000 from the firm, what was the increase or decrease in capital? If the withdrawal were $9,000 instead of $2,000, what would his increase or decrease be?

Case 3

Prepare a balance sheet of December 31, 2017 based on the data below:

Accounts Payable	$3,000	Supplies	$200
Cash	4,000	Net Income	11,400
Equipment	16,000	Drawing	10,200
Notes Payable	12,000	Capital, January	4,000

Case 4

The balance of the account of Dr. C. Moss, Psychologist, appears as follows:

Using the forms provided below, prepare: (a) an income statement, (b) a statement of owner's equity, and (c) a classified balance sheet.

Accounts Payable	$2,800	Accounts Receivable	$3,600
Building	12,000	Capital, January 1, 2011	1,900
Cash	12,200	Sales Revenue	3,8000
Drawing	6,000	Equipment	15,000
Furniture	3,000	Mortgage Payable	10,000
Miscellaneous Expense	2,000	Salaries Payable	2,000
Supplies	6,000	Salaries Expense	8,000
Supplies Expense	4,000		

Extended Reading

The Statement of Cash Flows

FASB statement No. 95 announces the new statement's official use in the system of financial statements. The statement No. 95 provides that the statement should be titled "The Statement of Cash Flows", which must be prepared on a cash basis. According to the statement, the cash in the statement includes not only cash itself but also short-term, highly liquid investments; that is, the concept is referred to the cash and cash equivalents.

The statement of cash flows classified cash inflows and cash outflows into operating, investing, and financing activities. In brief, operating activities involve income statement items, investing activities generally result from changes in long-term assets. Financing activities generally related to long-term liabilities and owner's equity items. The firms must use a fairly specific and detailed format to disclose the cash flows of the three categories. The statement of cash flows has many uses. The management may use the statement to determine dividend policy and cash-generating ability, and make relating decisions. The outside users, such as creditors and investors, may use it to judge the firm's profitability.

List of Reference Books

[1] 中华人民共和国财政部. 企业会计制度. 北京：经济科学出版社，2001.
[2] 葛军. 实用会计英语. 北京：高等教育出版社，2012.
[3] 耿晓兰. 会计英语. 北京：北京邮电大学出版社，2012.
[4] 常勋. 会计专业英语. 北京：机械工业出版社，2009.
[5] 全国会计专业技术资格考试领导小组. 中级会计实务. 北京：中国经济出版社，2013.
[6] 中华会计网校. http://www.chinaacc.com.